WITNESS COMMUNICATION TRAINING

Helping Witnesses Learn to Deliver and Defend the Truth Under Adverse Examination

Stuart Simon and Todd Betanzos
With Allan Campo

ISBN-13: 978-1533485496

ISBN-10: 1533485496

Contents:

Introduction

This book will help you to help your witness get prepared to testify. It is built upon a well-traveled training model: teach a communications concept, discuss the concept with the learner, create an immediate opportunity for the learner to put the concept into practice, provide feedback, then give the learner the opportunity to apply the concept again. Repeat several times.

You will come to see your role with witnesses in a new way. You will no longer be there to "prepare" a witness. You will be a facilitator for your witness, assisting him in preparing *himself* by helping him think about and communicate his Truth with precision and fullness. He will learn to listen to questions carefully and answer with care. He will also learn to respond appropriately when questions are poorly formed or misleading. He will politely and confidently reject that which is inaccurate or false. In short, he will be a complete witness.

This book owes much to our two works which preceded. The first, <u>Witness Preparation: A Manual for Attorneys</u> (2011) gives much that is foundational about our approach to helping a person get ready to testify. The second, <u>Hotseat: A Handbook For People who Face Tough Questions</u> (2014) is a book for witnesses and prospective witnesses. It should be read and re-read by anyone who is headed for the "hotseat".

As the title states, this is a training book. It contains a number of simple exercises that you and your prospective witness can use together to facilitate his learning. Several of the exercises were first described in the 2011 book <u>Witness Preparation: A Manual for Attorneys</u>, and are included here for completeness. Many of the exercises are preceded or followed by commentary that we hope you find helpful. We think you are best served when you can provide rich explanations to your witness about the concepts you want him to learn. That obliges us to try to provide rich explanations to *you.*

In hundreds of teaching sessions in virtually every state as well as in foreign venues, people have heard us expound on the three dimensions of testimony: The Truth, The Whole Truth, and Nothing But The Truth. If you have attended such a session, you know that we believe in anchoring the skills of giving good testimony in the Witness Oath: "I swear (or affirm) that the testimony I am about to give will be the truth, the whole truth, and nothing but the truth."

This book of exercises, like our instructional lectures and seminars, addresses these areas separately. The section on "The Truth" addresses how to speak to facts, what they are and are not, how to be precise, etc.. The section on "Whole Truth" explores the challenges of testifying about context and narrative; the things that give Truth its meaning. Finally, the exercises in the "Nothing But the Truth" section engage the task of sticking up for what you think to be True, and teach how to correctly reject that which is not.

Learn how to explain these concepts and how to do these exercises. You will become much more adept at helping witnesses prepare themselves to testify. You will be a better lawyer.

The Truth

Word Selection: Naming and Characterizing

The first principle we teach with regard to testimony is that speaking the truth requires precise language. Poets and writers of prose will search long and hard for the one word that captures the essence- the truth- about a flower or a sunrise or a person. You and your witness may need to do the same with his testimony.

It is easier to think about a thing when you have a word for it. It is easier to communicate about it, too. Sometimes we relate this story:

"I used to tell my kids that nobody ever bought cheeseburgers until somebody gave them a simple name. Why? In a very serious tone I would explain to them that it was very risky to walk into a restaurant and say that you wanted ""one-of-those-hot-ground-beef-patties-grilled-and-then-placed-on-a-round-bun-with-a-slice-of-cheddar-cheese-on-top-and-some-lettuce-and-tomato-and-ketchup-too! It was very easy for the person ordering to get part of that thirty-word formula wrong and end up with who knows what on a sandwich! It was also too easy for the person taking the order to miss one or two words of the order and prepare it incorrectly! Plus, everybody got really tired, just trying to order lunch…

Clearly, there was a need for a single unique word that immediately communicated everything the hungry customer wanted. It would need to be a word that the customer could give to an order-taker who then knew exactly what was being requested. Finally, along came a brilliant child who said, "Let's call it a 'cheeseburger'"! Ah… The world became a better place!

The kids loved the story and instantly saw the lesson. After all, kids are always asking, "What is that, Mom?", "What do you call that thing over there, Dad?" I bet your witness will get it, too.

The "Thesaurus" Exercise

Take five minutes and do this no-stress teaching drill with your witness. It will help to drive home for him the importance of word selection when seeking precision and accuracy in descriptive language. We usually call these terms "characterizations".

Ask him how many words or phrases he can think of that have more or less the same meaning as the word "nice" (with regard to a person). Offer him a dictionary or thesaurus as an aid. Then make a list together.

Here's some examples we found:

Nice: pleasant, likable, agreeable, personable, congenial, amiable, affable, genial, friendly, charming, delightful, engaging; sympathetic, simpatico, compassionate, good, polite, courteous, civil, refined, polished, genteel, elegant.

Now, ask him to think about a "nice" person he knows and request that he select the word from the list that captures the essence of that person's "nice-ness".

Notice how much more powerful- and accurate- it is to say of a friend who is notable for his kindness, for example, that he is "compassionate" rather than merely "nice". Both are one hundred percent true. But "nice" is general and non-specific, while "compassionate" captures the essence of the person. To describe him as "compassionate" is to speak to a listener with far more accuracy! That is what real testimony can be: finding the simple word that speaks to the essence of truth.

Brainstorm with your witness. What characterizations are needed in your case? Are there people who need to be described more thoughtfully, so as to capture their essence? Companies? Events? Places?

Doing the thesaurus exercise early in your preparation helps to put everyone (not just the witness!) into an alert frame of mind with regard to what things are being called and how they are being described. Your radar will be up for casual and, too often, less-than-accurate characterizations.

The "Titles" Exercise

It is typical in lawsuits to find one or more elements of the case that need to be called *something*. Sometimes an event is easier to talk about if it is named or given a title. That moment when two key individuals first come into one another's presence? Is it the "Introduction", the "Encounter", the "Discovery", the "Meeting", the "Confrontation"? What title most clearly captures the important qualities of the event? Figuring out and introducing useful names for case elements is a very worthwhile exercise for both attorneys and witnesses. These names help witnesses speak to the elements concisely and accurately; but, more importantly, names help listeners.

Listeners use names for events like the titles of chapters in a book; they are tools for organizing the story. The best ones are easy to remember, to carry around. We call this "portability". Good names and titles also pack rich imagery and help listeners recall the associated facts and arguments. We call this "capacity". A good event name or title has both portability and capacity.

Take five minutes and do this no-stress teaching drill with your witness. It will be enjoyable and will help to drive home the importance and the utility of names and titles for situations and events.

Ask your witness what comes to mind when these famous event titles are used:

"The Cold War"

"9/11"

"D-Day"

Notice together the richness of the imagery, how many things you and he can recall simply by bringing up the familiar title of something!

Now, ask your witness what comes to mind when he thinks of one of these common life-event names:

"My Graduation"

"My Wedding"

"My Best Vacation"

Notice again, how much detail and richness of imagery can come up for you simply by invoking the title of an event!

Many lawsuits (and almost all criminal cases) have one or more situations and/or events that would benefit from being named so that attorneys, witnesses, and fact-finders can organize and remember the associated information.

Brainstorm with your witness. What are the key moments in the story of your case? What are the key situations? What are the issues? What are the disagreements? Do these things need to be titled or named?

You add great power to your case if you (in voir dire or opening statement) or your witness (in testimony) are the first to assign names to objects, events, and/or situations; to label things. If you attach labels first, you will be able to assure that the titles and names of things capture their essence. You will be able to make sure that they are portable and capacious. We say to attorneys and witnesses: "If you name it- you can tame it." We also say, "If you name it- you can claim it."

Keep this idea in mind: If neither you nor your witness assign accurate and useful names to key events, situations, and objects (and arguments - arguments can be named, too!) somebody will. It might be opposing counsel, it might be a witness for the other side, it could be a juror. The name selected by another might mischaracterize the truth, unfairly color an event, or distort reality, and it might prove to be a key to persuading a fact-finder. Importantly, we also urge attorneys to use these names and titles in briefing, too. We want to give, not just the jury, but also the Trial Court useful word-tools for organizing and thinking about the issues in the case.

Sometimes one-word titles aren't sufficient to capture the real essence of the thing being named. For example, "accident" may not be enough. It may take "chain-reaction accident" or "high-speed accident" to deliver the full picture. If the essence of the event is not its dynamic so much as its effect, it might more truthfully be expressed as the "horrific accident" or (much different) that "unfortunate accident". Do not be tempted, through the use of such potent modifiers, to try to render a swan from an inescapably ugly duckling. Evocative adjectives and adverbs rarely work very well for listeners unless they help to drive home the truth. If they are used disingenuously, they typically ring sour, like a bad bell. Everybody hears it - and everybody grimaces.

Descriptive words in testimony are more effective when they are few in number and have been thoughtfully selected for their capacity to illuminate a point sincerely addressed. When thus used, they sparkle, and draw the listener's ear to the speaker's words. There is for the listener a reward: a flash of color, a surge of feeling.

The "Five W's" Exercise

Adding effective descriptive language is an important aid to bringing the truth into clear focus. Some stories, told too sparsely, fail to communicate their essence. One way to make sure that essence is addressed adequately is to think of what we term "The Five W's".

Controversy sometimes arises from focusing on a single element of and event as though that element was the only point of interest. Often the focus should be not on an event, but on its dynamics, upon its meaning, or upon the lesson it can teach us about something else.

Consider the following exercise:

Ask your witness to think of an issue in the case that created some controversy and make a list of the people involved and the actions taken (or not taken). Now, consider the first person on the list and address the "who, what, where, when, and why" with regard to him and his actions. Characterize each of the "who's", then the "what's", then the "where's, etc.

It should look and sound something like this:

Example of a First Event: "The sales representative lost a big client account"

Who: "The sales representative and a client" (Now, characterize the people in a way that captures the truth about them.)

The "inexperienced sales representative" and a "very demanding" client.

What: "There was a disagreement with the sales representative." (Now, characterize both the disagreement and the sales representative.)

An "unnecessary" disagreement between a "very demanding" client and the "inexperienced" sales rep.

Go on to the "where", "when, and "why" characterizations, continuing the pattern.

Notice how the characterizations begin to develop a story. This story seems to be developing an essence, an almost archetypal fable of youth and inexperience faltering in the face of a harsh business reality. This story's essence might be the lesson it teaches about the young salesperson's character, or the character of the customer. It might also be about forgiveness or about understanding. Notice how much richness you can inject into a story by attending to the "W's"!

A witness may fear that the descriptive language he uses to speak truthfully about something will be unlike that selected by others. You should explain that several people might notice quite different aspects of a person (or a thing, a situation, and event) and thus speak quite differently of it. Yet all are being absolutely honest and truthful. This reality isn't in and of itself problematic. What is problematic is when a witness lacks confidence in his own truth. Encourage your witness to feel confident about whatever is true for him. It is his Truth. He can use his words.

You may wish to tell your witnesses the parable of The Blind Men and the Elephant. It's a tale in which six blind men visit the palace of the Rajah and are given the opportunity to touch an elephant for the first time. This is a story about controversy arising because everyone is "blind" to the essence of the Truth.

Here is the moment as told by author Lillian Quigley in her children's book of the same name:

"The first blind man put out his hand and touched the side of the elephant. "How smooth! An elephant is like a wall." The second blind man put out his hand and touched the trunk of the elephant. "How round! An elephant is like a snake." The third blind man put out his hand and touched the tusk of the elephant. "How sharp! An elephant is like a spear." The fourth blind man put out his hand and touched the leg of the elephant. "How tall! An elephant is like a tree." The fifth blind man reached out his hand and touched the ear of the elephant. "How wide! An elephant is like a fan." The sixth blind man put out his hand and touched the tail of the elephant. "How thin! An elephant is like a rope.""

To continue the tale, there ensues a violent argument, as each insists the others are fools, or worse, liars. Finally, the wise Rajah explains that to find the real truth they must consolidate the things they know. They must put their findings together to discern the true nature of an elephant. That, of course, is just what it can be like in litigation, as the different perspectives (all truthful) of several of your witnesses are assembled to complete an overall picture.

Are there any elephants in your case waiting to be recognized? If you simultaneously look at the different perspectives of different witnesses, does a larger pattern emerge? The only way to find out is to get those perspectives side by side. Put them up on a flip chart. Taken as whole cloth, what larger story might they tell? If you can then look at that larger story together, you may realize some important truth, something greater in scope than the topic you *thought* was at hand. Even better, though, you will be able to help your witness see how his testimony fits in. He will worry less. He will have greater trust in his own truth and be more confident about the words he selects because he understands that his testimony is only a part of a greater narrative.

We will address a related issue later in this book. We will look at situations where a witness is asked to comment upon the actions, the writings, or the testimony of others.

Short Statements Tell it Best

Good witnesses give short answers. Short answers are clear answers. Short answers are easy to understand. The subject comes first, then the verb, then the object. The sentences contain no more than one or two descriptive terms.

Notice how the above section reads. The statements are written in the very style they espouse. It is not exciting reading, but it is clear and unambiguous. Your goal for your witness should be to have most of his testimony meet this standard. The judge and jury will appreciate it.

In the handbook, *Hotseat*, the reader is instructed as follows:

"Try as best you can to speak in short, simple sentences when answering questions in a testimony setting: Subject, verb, object - with only one or two characterizing (descriptive) words. Here's an example: Susan (subject) kissed (verb) Bob (object) passionately (descriptive). This simple style of speech will work best. It may sound awkward or boring to you, but your listeners will appreciate the clarity of your communication. You will make very few misstatements and the audience will not misunderstand you. Forcing yourself to speak in short sentences in this way will help you to organize your mind, too. You will have to focus upon how to describe specific things very clearly."

Most experienced litigation attorneys have seen and heard (too many times!) deposition testimony that is characterized by rambling, confusing answers to what are often simple questions. It is as though the witness is thinking aloud, wandering up and down the aisles of his mental storehouse, narrating as he goes, and creating confusion instead of clarity.

The lesson here is important. Long, complicated answers will simply not be remembered in their original form. Listeners will reduce them to short statements, perhaps even to short phrases, titles — sometimes even wordless images — in order to render them to a scale that can be comfortably kept in mind. You have no idea what short mental summaries might be created by listeners after hearing your witness produce a rambling compound-complex sentence. As noted earlier with regard to names, summary thoughts generated by listeners could be completely wrong. Inaccurate. Key elements may fall out of the message, lost on the cutting-room floor.

But, there is more to this problem. Speakers, too, drop elements out of long answers. Speakers forget where they started. They forget precisely what point they wanted to make. They introduce a key idea without all its parts because they can't keep them all in mind.

In terms of the testimony, less is usually more. The irony is that less is not merely more, less is usually also more likely to be accurate. Attempting to add more information frequently makes long answers less true because of some internal inaccuracy. The long answer may have missing elements or elements that are miscast.

Why? It's about the physical limitations of the brain. We explain to people that, at some point around twenty to thirty words into a long answer, they will simply be unable to remember what they said at the start. Their brains cannot hold such a long word sequence in short-term memory. Put simply, they will be lost, guided at best by some internal emotional compass. They will be looking for that *feeling* of being finished with their answer.

The way to prevent this problem is to help the testifier learn to present key facts and ideas in short form with useful titles and names for each important element. If delivered in a compact package, the listeners will appreciate and remember the message.

What follows are some exercises that can help your witness tune his ear to the length and clarity of his statements.

The "Dictation" Exercise

Ask your witness to answer some questions about the case as though he is dictating to a note-taker or secretary. It should sound something like this:

"Q. Mr. Anthony, can you tell the jury about your work?

A. "Certainly, I can period I am the Senior Vice President of Sales period My job is to get our product to market period I work with several vice presidents comma one for each region of the country comma in providing training and marketing resources to our sales representatives period"

Incidentally, this is a good example of what we have long called a "one, two, three answer" to an open-ended question. It's got the maximum number of facts a single answer should contain [3]. It delivers them in three short statements. And, it delivers them in the order that is easiest to remember. Read it again and notice the pattern: *"This is my job title. This is what I do. This is how I do it."* You should consider urging this three step package on most witnesses as they develop a short and accurate response to questions in the general category of "Tell the jury what you do for a living…".

As you can see, this exercise demands that a speaker listen to himself and monitor the structure of his statements. Most of us don't do this consciously unless we dictate a great deal. Consequently, many of us are lazy about sentence structure. Particularly, we are lazy about putting endings to our sentences! It usually doesn't take much of this type exchange for a long-winded witness to show marked improvement! Try it. It works.

The "Run-on" Exercise

Help your witness further improve his self-monitoring skills. Suggest that he answer your question, but this time *prohibit* the use of short statements. Insist that the entire answer be one long run-on sentence, with every clause joined to the next by a conjunction (a word that joins two clauses of a sentence) such as "and", "but", "if", or "so", etc.. It should sound something like this:

Q. "Mr. Anthony, can you tell the jury about your work?

A. "Certainly I can so I am the Senior Vice President of Sales and my job is to get our product to market so I work with several vice presidents and one for each region of the country and we're providing training and marketing resources for our sales representatives and…"

The answer can sound hilarious after only a few moments, but the lesson is nevertheless learned. Do a couple of rounds of these two exercises, alternating dictation-style answers with run-on answers to increase your witness' sensitivity to the length and structure of his statements.

Occasionally we have issued a written tongue-in-cheek "Conjunction Injunction" to a witness who over-uses connecting words like "but", "and" and "so"! We've handed one to the occasional attorney, too…

The "You Know" Exercise

Another big problem is frequent use of the space-filler "you know" in witness responses. You will hear many witnesses use "you know", "like", and "uh" as conjunctions! If your witness has this habit, get him to overuse the offending words intentionally as the only allowed joining term in his answer. This will increase his sensitivity to it. We have seen and heard many speakers abandon such terms after only one or two rounds of the "you know", or "you know, and" exercise!

Note that it is called the "You Know" exercise, but it should focus on whatever filler term your witness is using! If it's "and, uh", then do an "And, Uh" exercise.

The "You Know" exercise should sound something like this:

Q. "Mr. Anthony, can you tell the jury about your work?"

A. "Certainly I can you know I am the Senior Vice President of Sales you know and my job is to get our product to market you know and I work with several vice presidents you know one for each region of the country you know in providing training and marketing resources for you know our sales representatives."

Please take the time and trouble to do this if you have a witness with one of these annoying speech habits. Gap-filling words and phrases tend to appear more and more frequently in speech as people get more anxious. Most witnesses will be anxious at least some of the time during their testimony. If he's got an issue with this, help him. It is worth the effort!

Once your witness is thinking about communicating his truth in short, well-structured statements, give him some opportunities to do so. Ask him to state in just such statements the essence of events, situations, or issues with regard to your case. Listen carefully and challenge him to get the facts clear and accurate. He will have been thinking about the words that make the most sense for him and the characterizations that are important to help him correctly express his perspective. Now it is time to put them together.

Listen thoughtfully, with the ear of a juror. You can't tell your witness what the truth is, but you can tell him how he's doing at speaking the truth coherently. If he is pushed to communicate with precision in these exchanges with you, he will better learn to attend to clarity and accuracy. He will naturally recall terms that get him to his goal of delivering testimony with power and confidence. It will be his truth, well said.

Now, we have handled the basics. Let's get on to the interesting parts, learning how to keep facts in context. Later, we'll look at how a witness can "stick up" for his testimony; how he can learn to protect the truth.

The Whole Truth

Story, Background, and Context

In the handbook *Hotseat*, the reader is introduced to the following important concept:

> *"When another person tells us about something that happened to him, our sense of the meaning of that event is shaped by what we already know about that person and the circumstances in which the event happened. Knowing the background and context [the story] of an event helps us understand the whole truth about that event."*

Story, or, *narrative* - as we sometimes call it – is the full backdrop of any event. It is what gives events meaning. A "thing goes bump in the night" and any number of scenarios leap into our minds, depending on the backdrop against which it occurs. The backdrop story of a house with a sinking foundation? A neighbourhood troubled by burglaries? A child who is a restless sleeper? Been thinking about squirrels in the attic? Ever seen (or heard) teenagers playing scary games during an overnight sleepover? The possible interpretations of the "bump in the night" are as myriad as the narratives within which it can occur. It is the narrative that gives the "bump" its place in the world, its meaning.

Story includes all of the elements of the Whole Truth. It can explain about the character(s), has a plot, a setting, usually a conflict or problem, and an effort to resolve the conflict (often called *quest* by writers), and more.

When jurors and other fact-finders hear about events, they give them meaning by fitting them into a narrative structure, a story. All of us do it, all the time. It is how humans organize their recall for most experiences and the information related to experiences. You will find that we refer to "story", "narrative", "background", and "context" somewhat interchangeably in this book. But, you will know what we are talking about: the Whole Truth.

Earlier, we discussed giving titles to names and events. Just as importantly, it can help to think of your witness' testimony as a story-telling opportunity. What would be the title of the story he can tell? Who are the characters? What problem does he tell the jurors about? In the case of a medical expert, for example, the Title might be: "Solving the Mystery of Mr. Jones' Death". Your doctor expert best tells about it in a narrative.

"I first learned about this case by reading the coroner's report. What I immediately began wondering about was what ACTUALLY happened inside his heart in those last minutes…"

Testimony treated as narrative has a rich flavor. It is memorable. Witnesses feel secure when they have a story to tell rather than a handful of facts they are asked to report. Judges and juries organize the information better, too, aided by the narrative.

Help your witness arm himself with his facts integrated into a complete story so he can more meaningfully speak to the whole truth.

Let's talk first about factual background. "Background", as we use it here, means "history". Often there are key elements of your case that can only be correctly understood when set against the factual backdrop of a unique history. You will need to discuss this topic with your witness and help him be alert to questions he may be asked with regard to those key elements. The questioner may not address the history at all. The witness, in order to fulfil his oath to testify to the whole truth, will need to include the historical reference with his answer. To do otherwise risks inaccuracy and misunderstanding.

Remember the parable of "The Boy Who Cried 'Wolf'"? Tell this story to your witness as an example of the need for background in order to understand a situation:

"The Boy Who Cried Wolf" is an old folk tale about a young shepherd boy who became old enough to take his turn to guard the flock from predators. On his first night, he decided to tease the older shepherds by crying out, "Wolf!" as loudly as he could. This caused the shepherds to leave their beds and come running to his aid, believing that he needed help to keep the wolf away from their sheep. When they realized that it was a false alarm, they were upset with him and scolded him. But, he thought it was a great joke! He did it the next night and the next, making the other shepherds angrier and angrier. On the

fourth night the boy was on watch and a real wolf came hunting. The boy cried "Wolf!" at the top of his voice, but the jaded shepherds in the camp thought he was just teasing again and this time ignored him. The consequences were catastrophic.

Imagine the Supervising Shepherd being deposed some time after that terrible night. Notice that he hasn't learned to include the necessary background with his answer:

Q. "So, when young Billy cried "Wolf!", you didn't go and help him, did you?"

A. "No, Sir, I didn't."

Q. "You left him out there, didn't you? Just stayed in your warm bed, isn't that right?"

A. "Like I said, I didn't go."

Now, let's have the Supervising Shepherd make reference in his answers to the historical background. Notice how different this sounds when he points his answer towards the whole truth:

Q. "So, when young Billy cried "Wolf!" you didn't go and help him, did you?"

A. "That's right. Because of what happened before, we decided to not go."

Q. "You left him out there, didn't you? Just stayed in your warm bed, isn't that right?"

A. "Yes, Sir. It's sad, but we were trying to teach him an important lesson."

Earlier, we discussed how focusing on one aspect of an event can miss its essence. Here, the essence of the story lies in the state of mind of the Supervising Shepherd, *not* solely in what he did or didn't do. In order to speak to what was in his mind, he needs to tell the background story. This is not "explaining" every little thing gratuitously, as some witnesses are driven to do out of anxiety. This is calmly completing the story, so the truth can be told to the listener. The essential truth lies in the history that preceded the event, not in the event itself.

Later on, we'll take this idea even further as we look at questions of the "You didn't do X, did you?" variety in our section on Nothing But the Truth. As a preview, consider that, while someone is not doing "X", it may not mean they are doing *nothing*. It may well be that they are doing *something else*, something as good or better than "X".

Just as knowledge of the background of the case can be helpful to fact finders, so too can the knowledge of the personal background of the witness. In everyday life, it is by understanding someone's history that we make sense of his attitudes and behavior. Providing this same information can make a great deal of difference in the sometimes too-narrow universe of a lawsuit, and can help a jury understand choices the witness made.

The "Introducing The Answer" Exercise

Often the best way to deliver an answer which allows the telling of the whole truth is to make an introductory comment at the beginning of the answer. The comment should alert the listener as well as the questioner that the answer will require some elaboration. This introductory comment will usually have one of three effects upon the questioner.

The first and most desirable is that the questioner simply lets the witness give the complete answer because he (the questioner) doesn't want to appear to be obstructing the witness. The second is that he interrupts, but still asks the witness to explain, and *then* the witness gets to give his complete answer. The third, and you should help your witness to get ready for this, is that the questioner objects and demands a yes or no response, or simply ignores your witness' answer and goes on. This is *not* a problem. This is an *opportunity*.

If your witness has acquired some testifying acumen, he will look for a natural opening to re-visit the issue later in the examination when a question is asked on a similar or related topic. At the worst, he will have cued you to follow-up on the question in your later direct or re-direct examination. You can be sure, if the witness introduced the answer reasonably well, that the blank space in the story will be hanging there for all to see. If it is in a courtroom, both Judge and Jury will be waiting for that space to be filled.

Try this exercise with your witness as a way for him to learn to introduce answers which will require some elaboration.

Ask him a question about an issue in the case over which he is criticized for doing or not doing something, but which you and he believe he can explain if allowed. Then let him experiment with introducing his explanation.

One simple way to introduce an explanation in response to a yes-no question is to tell the questioner that the answer is "mostly yes" or "mostly no" or "partly yes and partly no" and then signal that there is more to the story. Make sure your witness knows how to do this, as it is a powerful technique for making sure he can get the whole truth into his answers.

Question: Tell me yes or no: you didn't create a safety policy for that location did you?

Answer: Well, partly yes-and partly no. *pause*

We certainly had a well-understood set of do's and don'ts there, but you are right that we didn't have a written policy document.

The pause is important, as it allows – or rather, forces – the questioner to decide whether to permit the elaborated answer. If he does nothing, the witness should proceed and complete the answer. About half of questioners will ask for the explanation. Another half (often more experienced) questioners will want to ask some sort of revised form of the original question in order to try to get the admission they are seeking. Usually that will leave the witness in more or less the same spot and another introduction can be made. ("Like I said, partly yes and partly no.") Now the questioner almost *has* to allow the explanation. To fail to do so puts the questioner at risk of appearing to be preventing the witness from answering.

Practice several times with this approach (and others illustrated below) to complex issues. Your witness will face many questions to which a mere "yes" or "no" response would fall far short of the truth. Make sure he can respond easily and gracefully. You will find that he is much more confident under fire when he doesn't feel boxed in by such limiting questions. He will know that he has the skill to manage the situation. He will be able to make sure he is allowed to testify to the whole truth.

Another way of introducing an answer is to explain that the question can't be answered with a "yes" or a "no". It might sound like this:

Question: Tell me yes or no: you didn't create a safety policy for that location did you?

Answer: I don't think I can answer that with a yes or a no. *pause*

You see, we had a policy, as we should have. What we didn't have was a policy document.

Some expert testifiers have told us that they sometimes introduce an elaborated answer by telling the questioner (and the audience of judge and jury) that they are glad he is asking about the topic. This, "I'm glad you are asking about this because it is important…" introduction positions the witness correctly to make whatever distinctions he thinks will best speak to the truth. It also alerts the listener that something of interest is about to be covered.

There are numerous elaborations on this theme, as you no doubt have already imagined. What is most important is that you give your witness the opportunity to learn to use this approach so that he can give complete testimony. It may not come to mind in the heat of adverse examination if he has not practiced it a few times.

We have come to understand that it is never enough to simply tell a witness how to manage a certain kind of question. Many, perhaps most, witnesses forget such advice more or less immediately. They have to train themselves to remember, and you have to help them do it. As said in the beginning of this book, repetition is the key.

Filling In the Context

There are two useful rules to follow to teach the truth about the people, objects, and events in a case. The first rule is to use accurate names and descriptive words that capture the essence of the thing named. The second rule has two parts: The first part is to give useful background information, usually in a narrative that teaches the listener how to think about the thing against the backdrop of history. The second part is to provide adequate context information; to teach about other people, objects, or events, usually existing concurrently, that affect the thing in question and that help to explain it. You and your witness may need to think and talk a lot about context.

More than once in any given deposition, or in testimony at trial, a question on an important point will demand a contextualized answer in order to be adequately answered. In other words, the answer is only the whole truth if it has all of its parts. Otherwise, it is less than whole, less than true. The best way for a witness to be confident that he can provide such answers is to have thought about and answered questions on the topic earlier. He will have already realized what needs to be told, and thought of words that aid in the most accurate telling.

Context is not merely color and flavor for a story. Frequently we find that the context IS the story, and we come to understand that the event which gave rise to a legal dipute is merely a blip on a much larger screen.

Learn to ask your witness for contextual information. You may very well discover other key dynamics that were at play during key events. There may be forces you will recognize to be relevant that the witness doesn't see as important, and thus won't think to tell you about unless you happen to ask. You've got to initiate the exploration and help the witness consider how things fit together. Contemplating these matters will help him speak to the whole truth when testifying.

In the handbook *Hotseat*, the reader learns the following:

"Remember, as people listen to you speak in response to a specific question, they are often putting together a bigger picture. They are inserting assumptions, making guesses, coming up with intuitive judgments about the complete truth. You make this much easier for them when you give them accurate context information to use in the process. You are helping them get to the whole truth.

Here are some examples of (personal) context information that can often help listeners learn the whole truth from your testimony:

Your health at the time in question.
Your family's health and circumstances.
Your mood and mindset at the time.
What you had been doing just before the time in question.
What you did just after that time.
What else is going on in proximity to you.
What other people were nearby, involved or not.

What was going on in the neighborhood, town, state, nation, world at the time."

You probably will profit from going through the above list with your witness.

You will learn that we prefer that witnesses be empowered to tell their affirmative story in adverse examination. Perhaps you have been trained in a different view. Perhaps you were taught to "save your story for trial" and thus have encouraged witnesses to *not* elaborate upon or explain their testimony in deposition. We learned it that way, too, but have come to see it differently.

There are several reasons we now urge that witnesses be prepared for deposition testimony as though they would be testifying as adverse witnesses at trial. That is, they are prepared to handle leading cross-examination type questions from a fully-informed perspective and are ready to give complete direct testimony. The most impactful witnesses, our studies have taught us, have learned to create opportunities to "tell their story" even while under adverse questioning. With the help of the exercises in this book, you can help *all* your witnesses become the kind of effective communicator that fact-finders listen to.

But, there are other advantages to having witnesses prepared to give complete answers to questions asked at deposition. Context is perhaps the most important one. A witness who has, with your help, thought about and prepared himself to discuss situations and events in correct context will be far more comfortable when he is asked out-of-context questions than a witness who is not as ready. Witness comfort is very important.

When a witness is asked out-of-context questions that he doesn't know how to handle, he will be bothered by the situation. He may become angry or anxious and begin to show some defensiveness or antagonism. He may begin over-thinking his answers. His mind may start racing, as he engages in internal speech and distracts himself even further. (We call this *"interference"*. Much more on this topic later!) In short, most of the possible outcomes of a witness not-knowing how to handle these out-of-context questions are negative ones. Neither you nor he wants that.

When witnesses are trying to answer questions out of context because they haven't thought enough about the context, or can't think of how to explain it, or just plain don't know it – they may actually begin to answer other questions in a way that is altered. Once the "conversation" gets out of context, everything that follows may be colored differently. It can be as though the entire exchange with opposing counsel is now going on in an out-of-kilter universe.

The easiest way to handle missing context is to let the attorney know it is missing and then put it into the testimony. Being able to do this makes witnesses feel great! They are confident and comfortable. Some science: Confident, comfortable witnesses are viewed as more credible. These exercises will help them get there.

The "Life History" Exercise

Take an hour or two or so to learn about your witness' life.

You should try to do it as a structured interview, asking about discreet periods in his life and then asking what major events happened in that period.

You should be interested in births, deaths, accidents, and moves from one place to another. You should learn what his parents' occupations were, major events for his parents that occurred while he was a child, memorable vacations, and about his best friends, etc.

You are likely to learn about events in his life that will help you understand him. This feeling of "knowing him" will improve your communication with him. You are also likely to learn things that inform you more deeply about his views of your case and his role in it.

Your interview should sound something like this:

Q. "Tell me a little about your parents. Where are they from, what were their occupations, and where did they live when you were born?

A. "I was born on a mountaintop in Tennessee…."

Q. "Now I want to ask you about several periods in your life and I'd like you to tell me the key facts about that period. Here's the kind of thing I'd like to know: I'm interested in births, deaths, moves, life changes for you, your parents, or other family members, and any key events you remember from that period. I want to know that about each period.

Q. "Let's start with early childhood years…

Then Elementary School Years
Adolescence: Junior High and High School
Early Adulthood: First job and/or college experiences

Subsequent Employment and/or Educational Experiences
Marriage or relationships w significant others"

Be systematic here. Be patient. Relax. Loosen your tie. Above all, listen carefully.

Obviously, exploring your witness' life is not meant to be an exhaustive process, nor is it counseling. It is getting to know someone well enough to understand who they are and how they come to be in the witness chair. Don't forget to ask follow-up questions! Learn more about that trip to Mexico when he was six years old, or why he quit playing baseball in high school.

For a variety of reasons, many attorneys resist the suggestion to explore their witness' personal history. Amazingly, the ones who resist the most will often later reverse themselves, declaring that this was the one of the most valuable things they did in preparing their witness for testimony.

Sometimes it is the witness who may be uncomfortable about an interview of this sort. For example, in defense situations in civil litigation, the witness may be a company employee who is not at all happy to be testifying and – especially if a former employee – may not be sure he even wants to testify in support of the company's defense. Such situations call for a gentle and very respectful touch.

First, make it clear that the only thing you will ever ask him to testify about is the truth, neither more nor less. He should not harbour any fear of being turned into a "mouthpiece". Further, think about doing what is described below before you try to go very far into the preparation. Here's a foretelling: Psychologists have long utilized personal disclosure as a tool for helping their clients open up to and trust them. It can work for lawyers, too!

Consider taking time to tell the witness your personal story before you ask for his. Tell him what kind of little kid you were. Then, with your own life narrative, "grow yourself up" right before his eyes into the lawyer he will be relying upon during his testimony. He will then have that feeling of "knowing" you. The result will be better rapport. He will be more likely to trust you.

The "Truth Circle" Exercise

Draw some circles on a note pad or flip chart. In the center circle, put the event or issue in question. What important things need to be understood by the judge and jury about the immediate time and place and topic? What must be addressed as though from that spot? Then go to the next circle out. What important things about the surrounding milieu need to be understood by judge and jury? In other words, what must be explained that is outside the event, but relevant to it? Then go to the next circle, the larger context of the witness' work and life, and go through the same process.

Example: Imagine a lawsuit about an accident involving a worker in a factory where your witness is employed. Your witness is being blamed for creating the conditions that caused the accident to happen.

The Truth Circle should include this:

Outer Circle - Life Context
Facts that teach about who your witness is; what he believes; how he does things.

Middle Circle - Indirect Context
Facts that that teach about the factory, the company, the witness' career, co-workers

Inner Circle – Immediate Context
Facts that immediately surround the event; who, what, when, where

A useful skill for a witness to acquire is to be able to introduce an answer to a question before actually delivering it. In the handbook *Hotseat* readers learn this:

"The next time you watch or listen to the news, pay attention to the way reporters work to put key context information into the front end of stories. Usually it's the intro that gives context and thus explains why the story is of interest.

Compare these two introductions:

Number 1: "In our next story, A Person walks Half a Mile to Borrow a Phone"

Huh? Who cares? Why should I be interested in this story? But, let's look at the second version which contains some provocative context information.

Number 2: "In our next story, A Blind Child Walks Half a Mile Cross-Country to Call 911 to get Help for His Sick Mother."

Wow! That context information makes the story nearly irresistible, doesn't it? You want to know what happened! Everyone does!

The objective fact that a person walked half a mile remains the same objective fact, of course. But that fact gets its real meaning from the context, the related facts which explain why it matters. Importantly, receiving the context information first helps the listener absorb and understand the complete picture. Otherwise, the risk of misunderstanding is increased.

Testifiers think a lot about context and background facts and how to say them clearly and concisely. They also learn to "introduce" their answers to questions with a provocative statement, not unlike the way a newscaster does."

We'll have even more for you on introducing answers later!

The "Missing Context" Exercise

Witnesses may expect to be asked about issues and events in a case in a logical order. They will often expect to be asked about their background first, their experiences in matters related to the case, then about events that preceded the key events in the case, etc. Unfortunately for witnesses with this expectation, attorneys often elect to ask about things in an order that seems illogical to a witness. The questioning attorney may focus a great deal on topics the witness finds to be unimportant or irrelevant. The questioning may also sometimes appear to be occurring in a vacuum, without the connections to place and time and circumstance that would help listeners to comprehend the full meaning of the exchange. This lack of such connection is the problem we attempt to address with the "Missing Context" Exercise.

It is important to understand that a topic taken up without any contextual introduction can create a very serious problem. When speakers introduce material without context, they leave the listeners to create their own connections. It is the natural process of the mind to set information in context. If no backdrop is given, then the listening mind *postulates* a context so as to make sense of what is being told. The problem is that the speaker has no idea what contextual elements the listener is applying and what meaning is thus being given to the information.

It is necessary to understand that the creation of context around a narrative is an automatic process. All listeners do it, all the time. Every time. They can't *not* do it.

When your witness is asked – and answers - questions about an event without having been first asked about the context, then the judge and jury will receive it in a stripped down form. What will they do? They will fill in the blanks for themselves just like any other human being would do! Judicial experience doesn't prevent it. Instructions to the jury from the Court don't prevent it. Nothing prevents it. The only thing which can forestall random blank-filling in the minds of the fact-finder is that the witness finds a way to get the context into the testimony.

Do the following exercise with your witness:

Select one or more of the events or issues in your case that must be examined in broad context in order to be understood. Imagine aloud with your witness what some questions might sound like if asked without context. Then talk together about what a listener would need to know in order to understand fully what had been asked about in the question.

Now, give your witness the opportunity to again hear and respond to those questions in a way that addresses the need for the missing context.

It might sound like this:

Question: It's true isn't it, that your company didn't set up a product development program for the Turbo-Widget?

Answer: Yes, that's true.

The above answer is technically correct, but the context-less environment allows the answer to deliver a false message. It needs to be handled another way.

(Below, the witness recognizes that the question has no background information to make it meaningful and that answering "Yes, that's true" without any context would send a false message about his company. He knows that the Turbo-Widget design is a well-known and well-trusted design in his industry. A product development program of the conventional type was unnecessary.)

Question: It's true isn't it, that your company didn't set up a product development program for the Turbo-Widget?

Answer: (Directly addressing the problem)

That's true, and you have to know the context to understand why we handled the Turbo-Widget that way.

Let's talk about something you may be thinking. Knowledgeable attorneys might worry that this type answer would draw an objection, since the question is essentially posed as a yes/no inquiry and the witness has given a two-part response. The "and you have to know…" might be regarded as non-responsive. Perhaps it might indeed draw an objection, and perhaps such an objection might be sustained; but for us that is purely a legal view. From a communications psychology perspective it is absolutely appropriate for the witness to address the missing context if his goal is to fulfill his oath of speaking the Truth and the Whole Truth.

To *seem* to be agreeing to something more than is actually asked will not feel right to a witness, and we thus encourage witnesses to raise it when they feel it. A trial Court might instruct a witness to answer yes or no, and the witness should of course defer when so instructed. Importantly, however, he has told the fact-finder he has a story to tell. He has let his own attorney know he is ready to deal with the topic on direct or re-direct if it is not covered further here. Perhaps most importantly, he has signaled strongly to the questioning attorney that he is ready to handle this line of questioning. The questioning attorney now has something to think about.

An alternative approach to answering might sound like this:

Question: It's true isn't it, that your company didn't set up a product development program for the Turbo-Widget?

Answer: I'm sorry. I'm not sure how to answer that because I don't know what product development context you are addressing.

(Here, the witness has thought about (in advance conversations with his attorney) the reality that the typical product development program is for new products, not products that were originally developed elsewhere, but that the company now manufactures. He realizes that the company has a different "development" approach to such migrant products. He's hoping to be asked to explain… The "context" the witness is referring to is "new product development" versus "migrated-from-elsewhere product development".)

The questioning attorney now has a decision to make. He can either ask what the witness is referring to and open the door for more direct testimony from the witness than the attorney wants, or, he must strike the question and go to another one.

You may also notice in this suggested answering style that it has a three-part formulation. In this case, it includes an apology, a "from-my-perspective" qualifier, and then a summary of the problem.

I'm sorry
I'm not sure I can answer
Because X is missing

We'll look even more carefully at the role of the apology and the from-my-perspective qualifier in a later exercise. You will want your witness to do these exercises and to learn to recognize that the apology is a powerful instrument of communication. As used in everyday conversation, it is a request for a courtesy which is rarely refused: "I apologize, but I don't quite understand." "I'm sorry, the question seems complicated." "Excuse me, can you ask that again." "Forgive me, but I don't quite get it." It serves equally as well in the more formal atmosphere of testimony.

Give your witness plenty of opportunities to practice organizing his responses utilizing this pattern. It will help him to better speak to the Truth.

Incomplete or Incorrect Questions

Incomplete information in the preamble to a question can create either a dilemma or an opportunity to your witness. Many questions asked by examining lawyers have elaborate preambles. Typically the preamble is a short speech that restates certain facts related to the question. Sometimes it is an attempt to lay a predicate in the legal sense, sometimes not. Often it is merely argument, an opportunity for the questioner to point out his favorite facts and restate his theme. Predicate or not, the preamble usually is colored in the way the questioning attorney prefers and includes references to only those facts which he wishes to connect to the question and the hoped-for answer. Your witness should learn to point out any missing facts in such questions.

Wait, isn't your witness supposed to "just answer the question"? Yes, of course he is. But, he can't answer a question that is inaccurate or which paints an inaccurate picture in its preamble. The preamble is part of the question. He should learn to say exactly that.

We tell witnesses that, when under oath, they *must* answer questions unless 1) their attorney instructs them not to answer on some legal ground or 2) the question is unanswerable as asked. The second point is the operative one for this discussion. Many witnesses attempt to answer questions that should by all rights be declared unanswerable. Often the question is merely confusing. Some questions are, as has been discussed earlier, "yes-no" questions that can't be answered with a "yes" or "no".

Witnesses should always be trying to answer questions as well as they can, but they have the right to expect lawyers to ask them questions that are complete and comprehensible. The lawyers, unfortunately, may not wish to do this. So, the witness may have to force the issue.

This should not be taken as a suggestion that you help your witness play games with questioners. That isn't right and it isn't the goal of this book or its authors, ever.

Questions with incomplete or incorrect preambles are in the class of unanswerable questions. The witness has the obligation is to answer with the Truth to all questions. But, how does he give a truthful answer to a question built upon a false or incomplete proposition expressed in its preamble? That is impossible. The solution to the dilemma is to identify the issue and get the question corrected. Then, the witness can be confident that his testimony is true and accurate, just as his oath requires, and as he will have to attest in writing.

The "Something's Missing in the Question" Exercise

Give your witness the opportunity to hear you develop several questions on case issues as they would likely be formulated by an opposing counsel. These questions should be similar in that all should have incomplete information in the preamble. There should be an important element of context omitted that goes directly to the point of the question. Point out to the witness what you have left out.

Then, let him practice listening to the questions again and responding in such a way that would oblige a questioner to either make a correction to the pending question or formulate a new one.

Question: So, you knew three years ago that you had this diagnosis, you knew the disease would worsen, and you knew you weren't getting any better – yet you never saw a cardiologist did you? It's correct, isn't it, that you never saw a cardiologist until very recently?

(Here, the witness has noticed that the missing ingredient in the preamble is that three different doctors told him there was no reason at the time to refer him to a cardiologist – and, so they didn't.)

Answer: No, that's not correct.

Question: Your answer is "No"? You're saying to this jury that it's not correct?

Answer: I'm sorry, I don't think I can agree that it's correct because there's something important missing in the question.

Now, of course, the questioner must decide what to do…

Please notice some things about the above style of answer. It has three basic and repeatable structural elements:

First, it begins with an apology. We've discussed their usefulness earlier, but, let's look further at apologies.

A witness who apologizes when he is having a problem with a question earns for himself the right to be treated with a reciprocal level of courtesy. In most instances, an appropriately courteous response will be given by the questioning attorney, especially if the session is videotaped. Why? If he does not respond with courtesy, the attorney risks appearing *on video* to be abusive or impolite. He will neither want the Court nor the jury to, literally, see him in a negative light.

In the next element of the answer, the witness frames it as "I don't *think* I can agree…" This might be called a "from-my-perspective" qualifier. This formulation is at once the most honest and, for that reason, the easiest to defend. The witness is speaking strictly about his own view, his own Truth. "I *think* something important is missing from the question, and *it doesn't make sense to me.*"

The "to me" part is thus important. To a Judge or jury, the question might sound completely reasonable. However, to the witness, it doesn't sound right at all because it postulates a situation he finds to be less than true. Less than true is only one thing – false. To agree by answering that the attorney is correct is to agree to a lie. But, the witness usually must explain what it is that is bothering him.

Finally, the key to the power of the "something important is missing" response is that the missing contextual element is *in fact* an important one. A question on this topic with this preamble should have that information in the preamble. The preamble without this key element is incomplete and the question is thus likely to misdirect a listener.

Tell your witness that the response should not imply that the attorney omitted the element on purpose. Perhaps he did and perhaps he didn't. But, just don't go there! The most courteous thing to do is to give the questioner the benefit of the doubt and play it straight. Our goal is not to "beat" opposing counsel. It is to get the witness a clear and complete question that allows him to make a truthful response that will not be misunderstood by a listener, whether arbitrator, judge, or jury.

Witnesses should not play games with this or any other of the techniques taught here. Our approach to testifying under adverse examination is not intended to urge a contest of wile and cunning between a witness and an attorney. Witnesses would usually lose such contests. Instead it is intended to empower witnesses with the understanding and the skill to confront bad questions head-on. And – it relies on upon an honest, courteous interactive style.

Help your witness to understand the three parts of this response and to get a feel for when and how to use it to structure an answer to a question. And, help him remember the underlying premise: This is a tool for speaking the Truth with precision and power. It is not a trick or a gimmick or a "technique".

I'm sorry
I don't think I can agree
There's something important missing

Do this with your witness half a dozen times with different questions on different topics and he will internalize the structure and begin to integrate it into his responses. His sense of the Truth will become clearer (even to him!) because it will be more accurately expressed.

Story: The "I Was There" Exercise

Now, since you are armed with the history of your witness and background factual information and contextual knowledge of every relevant level, it is time to tackle the Story.

Do this two-part exercise.

Part one is to speak with your witness about his overall story. Some folks like to use the metaphor of altitude, as in "What is your testimony all about if looked at from 10,000 feet (or 20,000 or 30,000). The idea is to get an overall concept for him (and you) to keep in mind. You might begin with something like, "Why are you needed to testify in this case?" That can be the beginning of his story.

Make sure you are both clear on what his perspective is. Fact witnesses generally have an "I was there" perspective. Frequently, 30(b)(6) witnesses have that perspective, too, but bring a unique institutional perspective as well. Experts have yet another perspective. Let's assume for now that you have a fact witness.

Talk with him about what he *wants* to tell people. If the witness were being asked by a youngster in junior high what his testimony was going to be about, what would he say? THAT might very well be the title of his story. "My testimony? I'm going there to tell them what it was like to work at Acme in 2005 and what it was like for all of us the day that tragic thing occurred."

"I was there" testimony can be very powerful. It has natural credibility for humans. We generally put trust in the story of the "eye witness" - unless he does something to cause us to doubt him. The way for your witness to get the full power of his unique perspective is to put it into a narrative that he can tell and with which the fact-finder can identify. The fact that he was there gives him an authority the questioning attorney can never match. The questioning attorney wasn't there and can't change that fact. Few questions, no matter how challenging, can quite surmount, "But, sir, I was THERE."

Remind your fact witness that he is testifying because *he was there*. He knows the things he knows because *he was there*. He can assert things strongly because *he was there*. He can stick up for himself because *he was there*. He knows what he saw, what he did and didn't do, and what he felt then and what he feels about it now. *He was there*. Because he was there, he can tell the whole story as he sees it.

In the second part of the exercise, ask your witness several questions in *adversarial mode* that beg a reference to this authority and to the overall story he is there to tell. He needs to be able to practice linking his mind to – and making reference to - this over-arching truth when asked such questions.

It might sound like this:

Question: "Since all we have is this disjointed testimony from three witnesses, nobody can really positively say what exactly happened there that day, can they?"

Answer: "I'm sorry. I can't agree to that. I was there and I *know* what happened."

Note that this answer begins with a polite apology. As we have reminded you often, the polite apology earns the witness at least some right to courtesy from the questioning attorney.

The second part of his answer includes the passive form of disagreement. He says, "I *can't* agree to that" rather than "I *won't* agree to that." *Can't* suggests that something is preventing agreement. It tells a listener that the witness would agree if he could, but he just *can't* because something is in the way. This is the polite form of disagreement; polite resistance to an unreasonable assertion.

The firmer-sounding "I *won't agree* can unintentionally communicate un-cooperativeness or, worse, arrogance. *Can't* is more accurate than *won't*, too. The reality should be that your witness enters the engagement entirely ready to agree with anything offered to him that is entirely true. But, if it is not entirely true, he *can't* agree. Period. He can't because his sworn oath demands that he testify to the truth, the whole truth, and nothing but the truth. Agreeing to something he doesn't think to be true would be failing to fulfill his obligation under his oath. He *can't* do that!

The "something" that is in the way is the authority of the witness's direct experience. He firmly says it, too: "I was there and I *know* what happened." He will like how it feels. You will like how it sounds.

Testifying about People

One of the most interesting challenges for witnesses is testifying about the actions of others. Even more challenging is testifying about what others have communicated in speech or in writing about why they did or did not do something. Let's look at these issues, starting with the issue of motive.

First things first. Human motivation is one of the hardest of all phenomena to understand and explain. None of us has *any idea* what causes the actions of other people. We may have theories. We may speculate. We may guess. But, we don't – and can't ever – know precisely why others do what they do. Even, and this is important, if they actually tell us "the reason" for something they did, we still cannot know if it is the only reason, or the main reason, or one of several equally compelling reasons. We know only what is communicated to us. How can we be confident that someone's explanation of a motive is correct, when we actually should be uncertain about our explanations of our *own* motives?

Psychologists and psychiatrists have long understood that people often get it completely wrong when they try to explain their reasons for certain behavior. The best most people can do is try to identify what they *think* might be the motive for doing something. That is because few of us can analyze our own feelings, thoughts, or behavior with much precision. Since few of us can analyze ourselves with precision, then few of us (probably far fewer!) can *explain* ourselves with precision. We know awfully little about our own inner self, and far, far less of others - including our closest friends and loved ones. That being said, we should approach with great care the matter of commenting upon the reasons behind the actions of others.

Even more subtle is the matter of describing the actions of others; of testifying about what they did or did not do.

Consider the following:

There was a call made by Bob to Jim. A message was left in Jim's voice-mail. There was no return call made to Bob.

Did Jim *fail* to return Bob's phone call? Did Jim *neglect* to return Bob's phone call? Did Jim *elect not* to return Bob's phone call? Did Jim *decide to defer* on a return call to Bob? Did Jim *do something other than* return Bob's phone call? Did Jim *not return* Bob's phone call?

Most of the verbs and verb phrases above arise from a theory of Jims' motives for any of his actions vis a vis Bob. The only one that may be argu-ably a neutral characterization is the last one. The point is that much of the descriptive language we use to speak about other people's actions is born from an implied understanding of their state of mind. We often have no such understanding! Actually, we *usually* have no such understanding! You will need to help your witness address this topic with accuracy (spelled T-R-U-T-H) in his testimony.

There may also be other important contextual aspects to the matter of what Jim did about that phone call. Let's imagine a few: Was it one of many calls? Was it concerning a topic that had already been handled? Were there email communications going on at the same time? Did someone else return Bob's call? Etc. Ideally, you will discuss "the phone call questions" with your witness and think about what contextual facts need to be included with his responses to such questions. But – for now – we are focused upon what he might truthfully and accurately say about what Jim did or didn't do and about what Jim's motives were.

The "How Did Jim Feel about That?" Exercise

Talk with your witness about any questions he may have to face with regard to the actions of others. Discuss with him the Truth with regard to their actions. Help him to recognize that he actually may have very little real knowledge about which he can be confident. Certainly he saw or heard whatever he saw or heard. He should think about and speak with you about how to describe that experience with accuracy. For your part, you should listen with great care for any *assumptions* he is adding into the story. You should challenge him very directly. Some of those assumptions could be dead wrong. Help him get better at not just trying to testify to the Truth as he believes it to be – but also to get better at recognizing what the Truth actually is.

Do the following two part exercise:

First, ask your witness direct-exam-style questions about the actions of another. Listen for how he describes and characterizes those actions. It might sound like this:

Question: "So, you saw Jim Johnson at the accident scene, didn't you? How was he reacting?"

Answer: "He wasn't doing anything. He was just standing there with a blank look on his face. That was his reaction."

Let's consider this answer. Your witness has agreed to describe how someone was "reacting". Reaction implies thoughts and feelings as well as action. How can your client possibly know all that?! The answer is, he can't. Further, he has elected to describe some moment as Jim "[not] doing anything", that he was "just standing there". Further, he chose to describe Jim's expression as a "blank look". The Truth is that all of these descriptions are interpretations, not actual reports of what was seen. This witness needs to think about what he actually saw. He needs to think about what the Whole Truth actually is.

After thinking about it more and speaking with you, a more accurate (thus Truthful) answer might sound like this:

Question: "So, you saw Jim Johnson at the accident scene, didn't you? How was he reacting?"

Answer: "I don't know how he was reacting internally, of course. At the moment I saw him, he appeared to be standing quietly and it looked to me like he was thinking."

Consider this answer: First this witness gives the important disclaimer that he doesn't know how Jim was "reacting". Then he describes what he saw in neutral language. He takes ownership of the descriptive language he has chosen by saying "he appeared to be standing quietly". This is pure Truth. The witness doesn't know what Jim was doing or not doing – he only knows how he appeared to the witness. Then, the witness does it again, taking responsibility for his stated impression that "it looked to me like he was thinking." This is very honest testimony and will make your witness feel strong and well-grounded when testifying.

Here's the second part of the exercise: After you have thought about and talked about what your witness can accurately say about Jim and Jim's actions, then ask him some questions in adversarial mode. Give him several opportunities to be very clear about the Whole Truth with regard to his knowledge of what others do and think and feel.

It may be that you (and your witness) feel that the truth would be best served by your witness being willing and able to characterize Jim and his actions. It must begin, of course, with your witness sincerely believing he can do it; that he knows enough about Jim or about the situation. There are some benefits to this approach, as it allows you and the witness to affirmatively inject language that may positively affect the case. If you want to think about doing this, we suggest you look again at the "Thesaurus Exercise" and work on this with your witness. On the other hand, you or your witness may not feel sure that you can or should even try to do such a thing. Either way can be correct. It depends on what your witness' sense of the Truth is, doesn't it?

The questions might sound like this:

Question: "So, how did Jim feel about the delays in payment on those materials?"

Answer: "I'm sorry, I can't answer that. I don't know how Jim felt."

Question: "But, you know that Jim stopped returning phone calls, don't you? You know he never spoke to the customer again, don't you?"

Answer: "I think I might characterize Jim's actions this way: He was working hard on the problems. He seemed to be looking for alternative ways to solve them. To me, Jim is an experienced professional and I would describe him as positively engaged with this issue. However, none of us know for sure what was in his mind. You'll have to ask Jim."

Or, if you have elected to NOT characterize Jim's actions.

Answer: "I can't characterize Jim's actions. As far as I know there were no additional conversations with the customer by any of us. But, I can't agree that it means Jim stopped returning calls or decided not to speak to the customer. I just don't know that. You'll have to ask Jim."

There are key elements to truthful and accurate responses to questions about the thoughts, feelings, and actions of others. Help your witness to learn to keep them in mind when asked questions of this type. The elements are slightly different when your witness (and you) believe he can tackle the assignment compared to when you believe it is best not to do so.

Here are both sets of elements:

1)

I think I might characterize Jim's actions this way: etc. etc. etc.
I think I would describe Jim this way: etc. etc. etc.
I certainly can't agree that Jim's action means what you (Mr. Attorney) say it means because I (and you) don't know what it means.

I just know how it seems to me
We have to ask Jim.

2)

I can't characterize another's actions.
I can only describe them.
I did observe X
I certainly can't agree that Jim's action means what you (Mr. Attorney) say it means because I (and you) don't know what it means.
We have to ask Jim.

As you examine the above patterns, notice that characterizing of the behavior or personal qualities of others should ALWAYS be owned as a personal judgment, not as verifiable fact. Your witness can only say truthfully what he *thinks* of the acts of others. If he stays true to this immutable truth, he will be far more credible. But, you must not only help him recognize the immutable truth on this matter, you must give him opportunities to practice thinking and speaking in this scrupulously precise way. You have to take time to ask him questions. He has to listen, think, and answer. Repeatedly.

Testifying about Documents

Answering questions about documents can be a daunting experience for a witness. There is much about the handling of such questions that is solely the product of skill and experience. Most of it will not come naturally. The witness will need to train himself to approach documents in a way that facilitates his delivering clear and accurate testimony about them.

Let's begin with how to physically handle a document when one is presented.

If your witness has been sitting correctly, he will have both forearms and hands on the table, with one hand resting lightly upon the other. He will be leaning slightly forward, have both feet upon the ground, his weight evenly distributed on his buttocks, and his head upright.

When he is handed a document, he should slide it into place in front of him in a position that makes it easy to read. He should, if possible, keep one forearm and hand anchored on the table while handling the document with the other. This will enable him to continue to keep a quiet and stable upper body.

If he needs to handle the document, turn it over, point something out, or move to a different page, he should try to do so in a slow methodical way. He should continue to try to keep his arms anchored by resting his elbows on the table as he handles the document.

It is easy to lose your place in a document. Your witness should always go slowly and double check where he is and what he is looking at.

When a document is placed before him, he will usually be asked to examine it and communicate if he recognizes it. Usually, it will at least appear to be a document you and he have looked at together as part of his preparation. It may already have been entered in the case and received a stamp and number. However, he should never assume that the document before him is the same as the one he looked at with you.

It is a two-step process: Verify the document first, then read it thoroughly.

When a witness receives a document, he should *request relief* in order to verify the document. He should say something like, "Let me just take a look at it, please." Or, "It looks familiar. However, please let me have a look so that I can be sure." Etc.

It is not enough to merely accept the document and begin checking it. A polite *request for relief* is needed. When a witness says something to the tune of, "Please let me check this to make sure it is what I think it is," he has created a circumstance where the questioning attorney must defer until he (the witness) actually says he is ready. To fail to defer until the witness is ready would be impolite at the least and might create complications the attorney would not want.

This practice of politely requesting relief to check documents, look at photographs, or even to think before answering a complex question will aid the witness even more at an actual hearing or trial.

Most documents should be completely re-read before answering questions about their contents. As confident as a witness may be that he knows, for example, an email "through and through", he may *still* become confused about it when questioned in the more intense situation of a deposition or trial.

After your witness has verified that he recognizes a document and that it appears to be complete, he should ask the attorney if the attorney is going to ask questions about the contents of the document. If the answer is in the affirmative, the witness should again politely *request relief* to read the document thoroughly. The attorney simply must comply with this request, as to fail to do so may have a cost he doesn't want to pay.

Sometimes questioning attorneys say, "You won't need to read it. I only have a couple of general questions." If this happens, your witness should be careful to guard the truth. Errors and mis-statements often happen when witnesses are asked such questions without refreshing themselves on the document.

General questions or not, the witness should have the document and its contents freshly in mind before answering *any* questions about it. He should learn to speak to it correctly and say something like, "No, I will not be fully confident in my answers if I can't first look at the document. So, please give me a minute to read it."

This is NOT a "maneuver". This is the Truth. He will be less sure of the accuracy of his answers if he doesn't first refresh his memory on the document.

Let's look at some document-related realities that your witness should understand. As is suggested by the note above, you and your witness should remember that there are certain things that are *always* true about documents and what can be said of them. Too many witnesses (too many attorneys, too) lose sight of these immutable facts.

It must always be acknowledged first that a document speaks for itself. It can be interpreted and commented upon by others, even by its author, but it still has its own voice, its own words. Once it is written, it stands on its own. If the words were ill-chosen, they cannot be undone. If they speak a truth that no-one wants to hear, they cannot be silenced. If they record a falsehood that cannot be disproven, then an opposite injury has been visited.

Thoughtful preparation on documents that contemplates these realities can make your witness not only a better testifier in the case at hand, but – if he writes letters and emails in the course of his business – he will become a more careful writer. In the modern era of electronic data handling and storage, words are forever. No email is personal and private. "Confidential" is a header on a page, not a protection of its contents. Casual text messages are forever embedded in databases as though carved into granite.

If documents speak for themselves, then what can your witness truthfully say about them? The answer is that he can't say much that is other than commentary, but he CAN give commentary of a type that is meaningful and useful to a fact-finder. This will only happen if he (the witness) thinks about the document from the right perspective and then speaks to it in clear language.

Thus, the essence of ALL testimony on documents is that it is made from the perspective of the witness as a *reader*. This is the Truth. His testimony is derived from what he thinks of and feels and remembers *when he reads the document*. This is a powerful place from which to testify and gives a witness a wide range from which he can point to the Truth as he sees it.

He does not ever have to know what the document "means". He – most of the time, anyway – *can't* ever know what any document means. He can only know what a specific line or phrase seems to be saying. He can only know what it causes him to recall. He can only know what *other* thoughts are invoked when he reads it. Once again, our mantra: This is the Truth.

The "What Does This Mean?" Exercise

Let's start training your witness in how to deal with questions on documents. As with many of our exercises, this one has two parts. It begins with you and your witness exploring the documents you think he may be questioned about.

First, you should identify the most important (usually only a handful) documents and make sure you speak about those documents repeatedly. Make sure you are not the only one who decides which documents should be treated as "important". There may be emails, for instance, about which your witness is worried or confused that you don't think are of any particular import. However, if they cause him concern you should treat them as important and make sure you cover them thoroughly and more than once. Put them in your "hot docs" pile!

Practicing with the "hot docs" first makes the work more manageable. In commercial civil cases of the type we encounter so often, there sometimes are so many documents that witnesses can get overwhelmed. Starting with and concentrating upon the key documents should reduce the initial stack to fewer than ten or so. It will be much less daunting.

Further, the document-testimony skills your witness will build in handling that small group of key items will be readily transferable to all those other documents. The confidence he acquires as he thinks about what he can honestly say about the most critical letters and other written items will also carry forward to the remaining materials. He will be less anxious. He will have more energy.

Select your first document and talk with your witness about what the document "is". Documents are often easier to handle if you give them a name or title. (Recall the "Titles Exercise" covered earlier in this book.) The name or title you use doesn't have to be written on the document! It can be a name you and your witness assign to the document that helps him remember what is important about it. The name should say something meaningful and true about the document. Importantly, well-chosen document names can invoke the context in which the document was authored and thus help the witness recall details that might otherwise slip from memory.

For example, a contract dated December 20, 2006 could be named "The '06 Contract". Or, it could be named "The Christmas Contract". It might be called "The Original Contract", or, alternatively, "The Amended Contract". It also could have a more symbolic name for your witness, such as "The Real Contract", or "John's Contract", or "The Bad Contract". The possibilities are boundless.

Naming a document will help a witness recall what is important about it. But, it will also help the fact-finder in a similar way. A witness may want to keep in mind how rushed the negotiations were at the end of the year and that some of the people in the negotiation were in a hurry to leave for holiday vacation. And, if he wants to remember how all of that hurrying and distraction caused the contract to have some unfortunate gaps, not noticed until later, he may want to call it "The Christmas Contract". The name *alone* will invoke the important context elements he wishes to communicate as part of his Whole Truth.

Your witness can refer to the document by this name during his testimony, of course, but that is only one use of this important communications tool. You can use the name, too, in briefing and other writings. You can use the name when you question other witnesses in the case. If it is a good name it will become part of the case, as though it was always spoken of in that way.

The name your witness selects because it expresses the truth for him thus can become a powerful factual anchor in the case. Imagine this: *"And, ladies and gentlemen, this story really began that fateful winter day; the day the Christmas Contract was signed...."*

Now, after deciding how you will refer to a document, speak with your witness about what he knows with regard to its writing and its contents. Try to cover this ground thoroughly, looking and listening carefully for the gaps in knowledge your witness will inevitably have and the guesses and assumptions he will inevitably use to fill those gaps. Point them out to him. Make him see them for what they are. Then, explain that recognizing and acknowledging the gaps is good news rather than bad.

This problem of gaps in knowledge will even occur if your witness was the author of the document. If the letter (for example) was written more than a few days ago, your witness will have already forgotten at least some of the surrounding facts and circumstances. Often, he will not be able to explain why he made a particular reference or chose a specific word. He simply won't remember. Like any other reader, he will be tempted to fill in those gaps, too, with guesses and assumptions. Point that out to him. Don't criticize. Just point it out.

Ultimately, your witness should arrive at a spot where he is clear on several things about the document. Generally, these are:

What to call it (a name or title)
What he actually knows about it
What he knows about related events and circumstances
What he is unsure about with regard to the document.
What he thinks of when he reads it as a complete document
What he thinks of when he reads certain key lines or passages
What is said of the document that he believes to be true
What is said of the document that he believes to be not true.

Now, let's do the second part of the exercise:

Ask your witness *in adversarial mode* questions that allow him to practice speaking about documents from the perspective of a reader of the document who is correctly offering as his testimony *only the truthful commentary* he can make as a reader.

It might sound like this:

Question: "Now that you've refreshed yourself on this email. Read that second paragraph and tell me what it means, please?"

Answer: "I'm sorry. If you're asking me what the writer of the letter meant, I can't tell you. I would only be guessing. I *can* go over what it says here by reading it to you, if you want me to."

Question: "Look, this is a straightforward question. The language doesn't look confusing, does it? What does it mean?"

Answer: "I'm sorry. Are you asking what it means to *me?* If so, I can tell you what comes up for me as I read it."

Question: "Look, don't these three sentences taken together show an intent to ignore the obligations of the contract?"

Answer: "As I said, I can't speak for the author of that letter, but I can't agree with that conclusion. I don't get that from it at all."

The above examples of answers illustrate ways for witnesses to address the essential truths. These essential truths should never be assumed to be obvious to the fact-finder. Jurors, for example, often need to be reminded that Mary can't have any idea why Judy wrote a specific letter on a specific day. Asking Mary what Judy meant is asking Mary to *guess under oath.* She should NEVER do that.

The answers also begin, as we urge over and over, with an apology.

"I'm sorry. I don't mean to delay. I understand my obligation to answer your questions. I want to answer your questions. But, I can't do that with this one."

Then the answer moves to a statement of the foundational truth.

"If I tried to tell you what he meant, that would be like I knew what was going on in his mind. I can't possibly know that. That's why I'm saying I can't tell you what he meant. I would be guessing. I can't guess under oath. That wouldn't be the Truth."

Then, the witness affirmatively asserts a willingness to testify to what he *can* know, that is what comes up for him when he reads the material in question.

"If you want me to tell you what comes into my mind (or, "…what I'm thinking when I read it, what pops up, my reaction, my impression, my feeling," etc.), then I can sure tell you that."

Finally, the witness states firmly his opposition to what the questioner has suggested about the meaning of the document. Since the witness has now gotten the conversation on the correct level (What a reasonable person **thinks** is being said in a writing.), he is free to express a view *with equal authority* to that of the questioner or anybody else except, perhaps, the author of the letter.

Here are the essential elements:

I'm sorry.
I can't tell you what the author meant
That would be guessing under oath.
I am absolutely ready to tell you what thoughts I have on it.
I can't at all agree with what *you* say it means.

Work with your witness on documents using this approach. You and he will be glad that you took the time to do it.

You may wonder how these rules apply to a document authored by the witness. Mostly they will apply in much the same way, as surprising as that may seem. That is because witnesses often cannot remember exactly what they were thinking or feeling when they authored a particular email, for example.

A witness may not remember all the contextual elements surrounding the writing of the letter. He may not remember phone calls or conversations which occurred just before or just after the letter was authored. He may not recall why he covered certain topics and not others. All of these memory gaps are normal. Your witness should not be worried or embarrassed about them. He should piece his memory together as best he can, staying true to his obligation to honesty and accuracy, then think about how to speak to the document.

To achieve rigorously true and accurate testimony, he may have to say things like:

I'm sorry

I'm not sure what I meant by that reference in my letter

I can tell you what comes up for me now when I read it

I have no information to tell me exactly what I was thinking so I could only guess if you asked me what it "meant"

I can't agree, though, with your conclusion about what I meant. It doesn't strike me that way at all.

Testifying about Beliefs and Viewpoints

Sometimes a witness just doesn't know why something was done or not done. He doesn't have actual direct knowledge, for example, of whether or not his colleague Mary ran the required status checks on the processing machines on a particular day. He can't confirm or disconfirm that the status checks were done on that date.

But, your witness can still testify in support of his colleague, as long as he sincerely believes she did those status checks. He must testify, not on observations he made, but on the *beliefs* derived from his knowledge of Mary and how she did her job. This is the fullness of context; of truth rounded out in its entirety.

If, from your witness's perspective, it would fall far short of the whole truth to agree that since it can't be verified that Mary did the status checks, there is NO reason to conclude that she did them. It may be that he instead thinks the whole truth is that he and others have seen Mary faithfully perform those status checks many times in the past and so he has confidence that she probably did the checks on the date in question. He should feel confident about his belief and be ready to confidently testify about it.

We have often said to attorneys, "If your witness cannot affirm an act, he may still be able to affirm the actor." Your witness can't verify the act of doing a status check on date X, but he *can* still stick up for Mary!

This principle also applies to situations in which your witness must stick up for *himself.* He may not be able to "prove" that he did or did not perform a certain action years ago, but he knows himself and how he does things. If he holds the sincere belief that he would have or would not have acted in a certain way, he should confidently testify to his belief.

Sincere belief arms witnesses in an important way. They are not stuck in the witness chair having to make "admissions" which they consider to be almost surely untrue. The whole truth *isn't* "I don't know." The whole truth is "I don't know - but I believe…"

Admitting that he "has no proof" that he locked his file cabinets up on August 4th, 2004 will feel desperately wrong to your witness if he *always* locked his file cabinets at the end of the day. If he firmly believes he locked them, then admitting to "having no proof" without adding the affirmative testimony about his own habits and practices would be agreeing to a half-truth. The *other half* of a half-truth is a *falsehood*.

Your witness, then, needs to know how to address the "personal proof" that arises from belief in himself or in another person. As we use the term, "personal proof" is not directly verifiable or directly known. It is *inferred* from what is known about a person or situation. It is enough for me to conclude something about a person's actions because I know the person and his actions very well. That is my personal proof. Attorneys might call it *circumstantial* proof.

Personal proof can lead to the formation of sincerely held viewpoints which can be testified about with similar (sometimes even *greater*) power than verifiable facts. The short form of such viewpoint formation is this:

I know Bob
I know Bob usually did X
I believe in Bob's character
I believe he did X on that day
I absolutely do not accept your assertion that because it isn't proven that he did it, then he must not have done it. I *believe* you're wrong about this.

Alternatively, the same elements apply to an "I know *me*" pattern of testimony.

I know me
I know I usually did X
I believe in myself
Etc.

The important thing is to neither try to elevate personal proof to the level of verifiable fact nor to make the opposite mistake and treat it as less valuable than harder evidence. Let it be what it is: *belief.* Belief matters. Belief and viewpoint are as relevant in the legal process as in real life.

The "I Don't Know, But I Believe" Exercise

Do this two-part exercise.

First: Think about and speak with your witness about any issues in your case where there is an absence of tangible evidence to support your and his view of things. Ask him to think aloud about it and to give you every basis for his belief that he can possibly call to mind.

You may notice that this exercise is similar in some ways to the "I Was There" exercise.

Don't evaluate or grade in any way the things that come up for the witness. Simply make note of them together and then discuss them. Sometimes a witness's reasons for believing something seem "silly" to him and he is uncomfortable voicing them. You, however, may recognize that there is more substance there than even the witness sees.

Belief doesn't always oblige rationality. Think of people you know who have said something like, "I can't put my finger on it, but there is something good in that guy that I have faith in." Such a statement is not based in verifiable fact. It is based in something intuitive.

Here's what matters: Intuitive bases for holding beliefs can be respected and appreciated and *relied upon* by fact-finders. Why? Because we *all* have at least some beliefs about others and about the world which are founded upon the irrational. We trust our beliefs nonetheless, don't we?

The second part of the exercise involves your witness learning how to testify about his beliefs and viewpoints. You should ask him in *adversarial mode* questions that allow him to learn to present his beliefs in a way that meets his obligation to rigorously adhere to the truth.

It might sound like this:

Question: "This accident occurred at two oclock in the morning, didn't it? You know, don't you, that Dr. Stewart has testified that fatigue was likely a factor in causing this tragedy?"

Answer: "I'm sorry. I have heard that Dr. Stewart said that, but I just can't accept it. I think he's wrong on this one."

Question: "So, you are so committed to your story that you are rejecting the testimony of one of the nation's experts on sleep deprivation – that's what you're doing aren't you?"

Answer: "Like I said, I'm sorry. But, I can't accept that sleep deprivation or fatigue was the problem because I knew Larry Jones. He wouldn't have let himself drive if he was that tired. That's what I believe."

Let's look at the way the elements of belief are handled here by our witness.

First, he begins with an apology. By now, you will have learned the power of opening with an apology. It is courteous – and it begs reciprocity.

Then the witness takes responsibility for what he is about to say. "I can't accept" and "I think he's wrong on this one" is a very accurate rending of the truth. This witness is not trying to make it more than that. It doesn't *need* to be more than that.

We usually urge witnesses to register their objection to a proposition in a question but not rush too quickly to an explanation. Make a firm denial of the sort illustrated above: "I think he's wrong on this one."

Let the questioning lawyer follow up on the matter – or fail to follow up. If he avoids further inquiry, it will be obvious to all. If he asks for more on the topic, then the witness's explanation for the basis of his belief will flow smoothly out.

When you teach your witness how to manage his way through adversarial questioning, try to go at it both ways when he says something like "He's wrong on this one." Follow up on some questions and let your witness make his belief-based explanation. But, be sure to let him know how it feels when the attorney *doesn't* follow up, too. There is sometimes a great "whoosh", as though all the air is sucked out of the room, when an attorney elects to ignore such an answer and goes on to another question. The witness can be left hanging; but, so are the judge and jury. A kind of disequilibrium can descend upon the scene. These can be big moments in testimony.

Nothing but the Truth

Gatekeeping

In the handbook, *Hotseat,* the reader learns this important lesson:

"The words you speak in the role of testifier should meet the strict test of being nothing but the truth. If there is controversy, though, your statements are likely to be challenged. You will probably have to defend and explain your view of things. You may also need to react honestly and truthfully to different or opposing views. Because of this, you frequently have to spend more energy preparing for questioning by opposing parties than for telling your story directly. Importantly, answering questions from someone with an opposing position requires that you have a good knowledge of their view of things. Depending upon your role in the story, you may need to be able to speak with the same thoughtfulness and clarity you will have brought to speaking your own truth to both the criticisms of your testimony and any contradictory testimony of others. There could be a lot of thinking to do."

Being deposed or cross-examined can be an excruciating experience for a witness. Witnesses who were committed to honesty and candor under oath and trying their best to deliver on that commitment, have time and again been eviscerated by skillful examiners. It is not the facts themselves that are the problem, nor the veracity of the witness. It is the harsh reality of the legal contest, where the winning instrument of play is as often the skillfully crafted question as the honestly delivered answer.

Your energies, like that of your witness will thus need to be directed as much or more to preparing for the questions as for the answers. The rules of adverse examination favor the questioner. You can help your witness gain a significant measure of control by first helping him understand those rules.

In *Hotseat,* the reader sees this:

"In general, the rules for a testifier in a question-answer situation are these:

You must speak only the truth.

You should not refuse to answer a question (unless it would be legally improper to answer).

The questioner decides what topics will be covered and in what order.

The questioner decides how to structure the questions.

The questioner decides what terms and characterizations to use in the questions.

The questioner decides what, if any, propositions are built into the questions."

Your witness will need you to teach him how to deal with challenging questions. Dealing with the unique questions and questioning patterns of litigation obliges a witness to learn *Gatekeeping*. For us, gatekeeping is what a witness has to do in order to protect the truth, to guard the integrity of his testimony.

Teaching gatekeeping to your witness is a matter of facilitating the acquisition of certain competencies and thus involves more than imparting information. It requires actual training in the necessary witness communication skills that are specific to the unique situations of deposition and cross-examination. Training, as we use the term, involves learning about and then actually practicing the use of the skills. It is, as we will repeat more than once, *learning by doing*.

Most of what remains in this book addresses training a prospective witness in the art of gatekeeping: learning how to protect the truth as he understands it. As in the earlier sections, we will suggest exercises you can do with your witness, integrated into the course of your preparation, that will help him to develop the skills he will need.

Listening Comes First

Knowing when and how to answer adverse questions obliges careful attention. Your witness must learn how to deal with all types of questions. In order to deal with them, he has to first learn how to *listen* to them.

We know that frequently people do not listen to the entirety of a question. They seem to listen for the general subject of the question, then reply intuitively to what they judge to be the thrust of it, rather than composing an answer that matches the specifics of the inquiry. In ordinary conversation this type of approximated response is often accepted as satisfactory.

For example: A polite, "How's your Mama?" to a friend might elicit a story about the friend's Mama having surgery. But, it also might get the questioner a story about Mama's recent argument with a neighbor, or about Mama's new hobby, etc. The questioner may or may not follow up. After all, it's just conversation. Giving testimony, your witness must understand, is NOT just conversation.

Pace

Questions can rarely be too short or delivered too slowly. Almost all problems are in the opposite direction.

If the questioning pace is too fast, your witness will need to know that he can ask the questioner to slow down. Sometimes the questioning attorney simply speaks at a rapid rate, and the questions themselves are hard to follow. If that's the case, your witness should know how to say something like this: "I want to make sure I understand your question, but you are speaking a bit too fast for me. Would you please slow down?" Now you have it in the record. You should intervene in your witness' behalf if it happens again.

The other problem related to pace is when one question rushes in so quickly behind another that the witness has no time to gather himself, to have a sip of water, or take a breath. Once again, he should know that he can say something about it. Something like, "Give me a moment, please. I want to clear my mind so that I can listen to your next question."

The goal is for your witness to testify to the truth. If a question is rushed at him while he is still collecting his thoughts from the question preceding, he may misunderstand and respond in a way that is confusing or incorrect. He's not asking for special treatment, he's asking to be given the opportunity to fulfil his oath.

If questions are too long, your witness may have trouble keeping clear on what is being asked. As discussed earlier with regard to the "Repeat the Question" exercise, he should always be able to recite a question back word-for-word. If he can't do so, it is often because the question is simply too long. If it is too long to remember, it will be of necessity reduced to summary thought in the witness' brain. The risk of miscommunication with the questioner then becomes very real.

Interference

Hopefully you will have read and given to your witness a copy of the witness handbook, *Hotseat.* If so, you will be familiar with the concept of *interference.*

Recall that here's how we introduce prospective witnesses to the concept in Hotseat:

"A ▢ source of difficulty, and one that is under-estimated, is what is sometimes called "interference". Perhaps you can recall a time when you heard buzzing and static in your cell phone because of electronic waves emitting from some nearby machine. That buzzing and static "interfered" with your cell phone signal. It was harder to communicate, wasn't it? If the noise was loud or the tone irritating, it may even have been hard to think. Interference "noise" can happen inside your head, also, when a thought is distracting you so much that you can't think very well. Interference is a common problem for witnesses during testimony…"

You have seen it and heard about it, though you may not have known it by its name. You have almost surely experienced it yourself during some difficult conversation. You may have experienced it under the pressure of oral argument at a hearing, when a Trial Court asked you questions and something suddenly came up for you that created a distracting noise in your head. It was a thought that wouldn't go away or perhaps it was an irritating little voice in the back of your brain that chattered away while you were trying to think. That was interference. You didn't like it. Your witness won't like it either.

There are several common forms of interference encountered by most witnesses at one time or another. Each can be thought of as an inner voice announcing its distress. Often the witness experiencing the interference doesn't realize that he is probably sub-vocalizing and talking to himself about what is happening until you point it out. He may experience it instead as just an uncomfortable feeling of distraction and an inner mental busy-ness. A closer examination, though, usually reveals some amount of "talking to himself" during the questioning by the opposing lawyer. That inner talk *interferes* with his concentration. It can reduce his ability to clearly and accurately communicate the Truth.

We have found that the inner speech of interference tends to be similar for everyone, no matter their age, background, or experience with testimony. Here's what a few common interference announcements sound like:

"I am so nervous. I don't want to mess up here and get in trouble!"

"I am so angry. I hate this guy!"

"Oh my gosh, I wasn't prepared for this line of questions!"

"I'm stupid! I can't follow these questions!"

"Oh, no! I think I just contradicted myself!"

"That's weird. He didn't ask me anything else on that topic!"

"That sounds a little strange. Why is he saying it like that?"

"I didn't know about X. That means he might be right and I'm the one that's wrong!"

"I'm feeling confused and can't think clearly!"

Once one of these negative mantras gets going in the brain of a witness, it can go on and on and get louder and louder. Witnesses need to know what to do.

In the upcoming material, we will work hard on gatekeeping techniques that both protect the truth AND help the witness with any interference that may come up.

"Answerable Questions"

Stress to your witness that he need not feel powerless when being questioned by an opposing attorney. His power is born from two well-established legal realities: (1) The witness has the right to an answerable question and (2) the witness has the right to give complete answers. Most attorneys and witnesses focus on the latter. But that is only half of the battle.

It is assuring themselves answerable questions that witnesses usually must learn from the beginning, with cumulative skill building lessons such as the ones taught here. The good news is that it doesn't take long for most people to catch on to these ideas. Once they attain some mastery over the questions, they will become much more effective with the answers.

What are the qualities of an answerable question? From the layman's perspective, they are these:

An answerable question is audible and delivered at a pace the witness can follow.

An answerable question is one the witness can hold in mind. It is not too long.

An answerable question is one that is comprehensible. It is not illogical.

An answerable question is one that is grammatically correct in its structure.

An answerable question in one that is free of inaccurate or incorrect assumptions.

An answerable question does not oblige a witness to agree to factual errors or inaccurate characterizations.

An answerable question does not oblige a witness to agree to a half-truth.

Well-prepared witnesses notice when a question has any of the above flaws and usually don't attempt to answer the as-asked question. Your witness can learn to do this, too.

Bad Questions are Not The Witness's Problem

Here's an important rule of thumb: If a witness cannot hold the question and all its parts clearly in mind and be confident he understands every word of it, he should not be expected to answer it. More importantly, he usually should not attempt to answer it, even if he thinks he has the "gist" of it. The chance of misunderstanding the question is very high in this scenario, and he should proceed carefully if he is to fulfil his duty to the truth. A useful way to develop a sensitive ear for bad questions is to do the listening exercises that follow.

You will want to stress to your witnesses that these listening exercises matter a great deal because the best testifiers are the best listeners. The best testifiers understand that a witness can gain a significant amount of control over the style of questions he gets. But, it all starts with paying careful attention to the questions! Listening come first.

Teach this important proposition: Doing something about a question that is hard to follow is the lawyer's responsibility, not that of your witness. If the lawyer can't or won't compose a question that is comprehensible, then there is no question to answer.

The witness must answer a question posed to him under oath unless 1) it is a legally improper one or 2) if he cannot answer.

In the first case you will instruct him not to answer. In the second, he must inform the questioning attorney that he cannot answer the question.

Let's look at an example: In the scenario we are considering here, the problem is that the question is too long to hold in mind and the witness cannot be sure he grasps it in its entirety.

It is important for all witnesses to be comfortable with the assertion of their right to be asked an *answerable* question. They don't have to accept a question that is too long. The goal is helping witnesses adhere precisely to the truth. They cannot be confident that they are doing this if the question creates uncertainty by its length and complexity. They should not attempt an answer. They should politely challenge the question.

You will want to help them to know how to do it. First, teach the basic statements a witness can make when such a question is posed.

"I'm sorry, the question seems very long, can you shorten it for me?"

"Excuse me, I am not confident that I follow the question because it is somewhat long. Will you please shorten it?"

"I am not sure I can hold your entire question in mind. Will you please shorten it for me, or ask me a different question?"

Questioners often will respond by asking the question again in exactly the same way and with the same number of words. Your witness should not retreat. If the question was too long the first time it was asked, it is still too long the second time! Help your witness to understand that he can and should courteously push it back again. If it gets asked exactly the same way a third time, you should probably intervene in his behalf.

This situation could also be creating interference for your witness. This mental "noise" can be almost debilitating. However, the good news is that it can be handled with training that won't take long to do. We'll cover it at length in a later section.

The "Repeat the Question" Exercise

This exercise has two parts, the first is to simply give the witness practice at repeating a question to himself to be sure that he heard it correctly and can hold it in mind. You want your witness to acquire this skill. He will need to be able to sub-vocally repeat questions to himself during his actual examination whenever he is not sure he understands them. The way to practice this is to first repeat ALL questions *aloud*.

The second part of this exercise involves trying to get your witness to the limits of his capacity for short-term retention. He will probably only be able to repeat with perfect accuracy a question of twenty words or so. Even shorter questions can be hard to repeat if they have new or unusual words in them or several elements of data. You will want to create an experience of confusion and uncertainty for him that is caused by a question that is just too long and/or has too much "stuff" in it. However, try to make sure that this confusion is lighthearted and the topic innocuous so that the learning is enjoyable. The point will still be made.

Ask your witness a series of questions about anything: his job, sports, the weather. Start with short questions, move to lengthier ones, then to compound questions, and finally to compound-complex questions. For the purposes of this first exercise, make the questions closed-ended and factually correct. Don't put any tricky references or mischaracterizations in, as that will add too much complexity to this exercise. (You can do that later!) For now, make the questions all straightforward "yes-no" questions.

Tell your witness you don't want a question answered until after he repeats it back to you verbatim. Only then may he answer the question. Make a game of it at first by, for example, inserting a small amount of data into a simple question to make it fun and more challenging. (unfamiliar names, sports scores, phone numbers, scientific terms).

It should sound something like this:

Q. "Did you see the Reds' game last night?"
A. "Did (I) see the Reds' game last night?" "Yes."

Q. "Did you see that the Reds' won by a score of 9 to 4?"
A. "Did (I) see that the Reds' won by a score of 9 to 4?' "Yes."

Q. "Did you see that the Reds' also had 13 hits and only 1 error?"

A. "Did (I) see that the Reds' also had 13 hits and only 1 error?" "No, I didn't notice that."

Let's jump a few steps down the line:

Q. "Did you realize that, because the second baseman had a sore left shoulder, they were playing him closer to the bag, and that was the reason he couldn't get to the line drive that Lopez hit into short right field in the 8th inning?"

A. "Huh? Can you break that down?"

Now we are getting somewhere! This exercise has more to it than just getting witnesses to listen carefully to words. It also can show the difficulty of holding a compound-complex question clearly in mind so as to answer it. For now, you only want to accomplish one simple thing with this exercise. That is to help your witness recognize that "Huh?" feeling.

Silence Is Your Friend

Occasionally a questioning attorney will sit in silence after a witness has expressed difficulty with a question. Witnesses often get very uncomfortable when this occurs. Tell your witness to relax!

You should explain to your witness that periods of silence during a deposition are normal. In fact, silent stretches create a chance to take a deep breath, have a drink of water, or perhaps even stand up for a moment and stretch.

The witness should scrupulously avoid the temptation to fill silence. Many attorneys will wait quietly after a response from a witness; waiting for him to add something to his answer or amend it in some way. The witness should learn not to be drawn in.

If an answer wasn't enough for the attorney, he must ask for more. If he doesn't ask, the witness need not offer. Silence can be the witness' friend. Dead spots in the examination are the attorney's responsibility. The witness should sit quietly and let the attorney decide what he will ask about next.

Silence Training: The "Quizzical Look" Exercise

This is a short little exercise that is really worth the effort, especially if your witness is one of those people who has trouble with the silent period between questions. Often the problem is not the silence itself, but the "bait" created by the questioning attorney's facial expression. This exercise thus focuses upon expression, the real trigger, not upon silence.

We call this the "Quizzical Look" Exercise, but it could just as well be named after skeptical looks, or contemptuous looks, or stares, etc. These various facial-expression maneuvers are the stock-in-trade of many experienced attorneys and work by luring witnesses into rambling extensions of what usually began as entirely adequate answers to questions.

The witness is responding not to a request for more information, but to a *feeling* he gets when he sees the look on the face of the questioner. Often the witness is not conscious that he is reacting. It is an emotional event, a feeling he may not even consciously notice as he's experiencing it. The feeling can be anxiety, anger, or frustration. Or, it can be something positive, such as a genuine (though usually mistaken) wish to help the questioning lawyer "understand".

You can usually deal with this in about ten minutes of training. But, as with most of the lessons in this book, you won't deal with it by merely reading this section and then explaining it to him.

You have to instead help him notice when it's happening AS it's happening. That is the secret of adding communication training to your witness preparation. It becomes *learning by doing*. Once you let your witness "learn and do" this (or almost any of the skills taught in these pages) a handful of times, he will have far greater control over this typically involuntary unconscious response.

Do this simple exercise with a half-dozen questions on almost any topic:

This is a very good exercise to do with some kind of video, even if it's just a cell phone. It is in some sense an exercise for the witness's eyes rather than his ears. Record his reaction to the silence, then watch it together.

Explain to your witness what you will be doing and then ask him a question in *adversarial mode* and after he answers, sit there in absolute silence and, holding your body motionless, just look straight at him. It should go something like this:

Question: "Mr. Jones, it's your testimony that you and your colleagues did everything right that day, every single thing, not one tiny bit of anything wrong – am I correct on that?"

Answer: "Yes, sir. That's absolutely correct."

Now, sit there motionless and just stare at him, looking directly into his eyes. Hold onto that for about 10-20 seconds (which will seem interminable!).

Now discuss with him how he felt and how he looked to you *(or how he looked on the video)*. If he has been jumping in to fill silence in earlier prep sessions with you, he will probably tell you he found it uncomfortable or nerve-wracking or something of the sort. Just talk about it. Then do it again. Do it several times so that he can learn to feel it when silence is about to "push his button".

After he has learned to feel that button-pushing coming on, he can learn to say something to himself that reminds him to stay calm and quiet. He might say, "Oh, boy! Silence!", to remind himself that a quiet break can be just that, a break. Or he could say, "Ahh, the 'Silence Game'. I recognize this!", or some variation on this theme. Saying *something* to himself is important, though, as an affirmative sub-vocalization of recognition seems to really help most witnesses navigate this type situation more smoothly.

We'll discuss the power of sub-vocalization ("talking to yourself") much more as we move forward and discuss the concept of *interference*. Interference (a kind of distracting "noise" in the mind of the witness) can often involve negative sub-vocalization, the opposite of that discussed in the above paragraph.

Another variation on the silence theme is the asking of a softly sarcastic follow-up question that might sound something like this:

Question: "Mr. Jones, it's your testimony that you and your colleagues did everything right that day, every single thing, not one tiny bit of anything wrong – am I correct on that?"

Answer: "Yes, sir. That's absolutely correct."

Question: "You're really going to stick with that?"
Or, "That's it? No explanation?"

Help your witness get comfortable with such "questions". They don't deserve a response. They are not questions. They are merely argument of the cheapest sort.

You may wish to tell your witness that you will object if the questioning attorney pulls the sarcastic-question trick out of his bag. But, you still want your witness to have practiced remaining calm and comfortable when and if it happens. He can learn to just sit there peacefully and look back at the questioner, waiting for whatever is to come next. The table has been turned.

Forced Choice "Yes/No" Questions:

Forced-choice "Yes or No" questions are a device that often stymies witnesses who have not been taught how to handle them. In *Hotseat*, the reader learns this:

"Forced-choice questions are questions that are designed to limit the options of the person answering. As the name implies, you have to make a decision, you are forced to choose, usually between two positions. Forced-choice questions have great utility in the worlds of science and mathematics and philosophy. For the same reasons, they also have some utility in testing the truth of a statement or the strength of a position, as they may compel clear thought AND clear speech in both the person asking and the person answering. A proposition is positioned as a question and you must accept or reject it, agree or disagree. That seems okay, doesn't it? But, what happens in the real world?

What happens is that testifiers get asked these yes/no questions and just don't believe they can really be answered with a simple yes or no. Sometimes they get asked these questions and think the answer is something close to yes, or close to no, but not always- not all the time. They don't know what to do. But, you will know what to do. You will understand that you should not answer, "Yes." if the answer should actually be "Most of the time- yes". Your assignment is to answer accurately. Be very clear on the essential premise: "Yes", and "Most of the time-yes" are different. That is the whole truth and nothing but the truth.

Many times, you just can't answer a question with a simple yes/no or agree/disagree. If that is the case, you should say so - because that is the truth. Do not be afraid that you will be seen as impolite or difficult. If you are sincerely trying to get it right, your efforts will be appreciated and understood by most listeners."

Explore the following material with your witness. It will help him internalize a valuable concept that all testifiers should understand.

The "Three Dimensions of Yes and No"

When someone asserts a yes/no or agree/disagree proposition with us, we have a wide range of choices available to help us make an accurate response. Generally, we have three dimensions of the affirmative and three dimensions of the negative.

Absolute Yes and No: The central dimension, and the "choice" typically being "forced" by a questioner is that of the absolute affirmative or absolute negative with regard to the "true-ness" of a posited objective fact. This is usually stated flatly as "Yes" or "No" and applies itself best to observable, verifiable realities. To most listeners this means "X" or "O", the switch is "off" or it is "on", the room is either light or it is dark. No exception. Period.

Once asserted, an absolute can then be used to fence a witness in, to further limit his testimony. For that reason the absolute response is coveted by many attorneys, and they will work long and late constructing questions designed to elicit it. But, too often, witnesses who don't know what to do with such a question will answer in the absolute when it just isn't true. The attorney gets his prize, but it is undeserved. The witness got trapped by the demands of the question, not by the truth of the proposition asserted.

Limited Yes and No: The reality is that the answer to many questions posed as yes/no absolutes is something in-between the full affirmative and the full negative, and usually not even squarely in-between. Here, then, is our second dimension, the world of affirmative or negative responses that must be limited in some way, defined, or placed on a continuum. "What you have asserted, Mr. Attorney, is true, but only in a certain way".

Amplified Yes and No: Finally, there is the third dimension; an interesting one, too. Some proportion of forced-choice questions are designed, not merely to establish a fact, but to establish moral leverage ("You believe that people should be honest with each other, don't you?") with a witness. Or they are intended as pseudo-logical traps, baited and set in anticipation of a later inquiry. They can be tossed out as oh-by-the-way questions ("Before we start on this next topic- you agree that water is wet, don't you?") that are dripping with danger, should the witness hesitate even a moment in the answering. You will want your witness to know how to handle such questions.

Here are some examples of the former, some limited affirmatives, each placing the limitation in a slightly different spot on a continuum. These are "I agree" answers.

- Occasionally that's true
- Sometimes that's the case
- That's often how it is
- Correct, it's typically that way
- The majority of the time, right
- Almost always, that's correct
- Yes, that's accurate

Compare those examples to these "I don't agree" limited negatives:

- That's not a typical situation
- It's not usually that way
- That's hardly ever true
- That's an extremely rare scenario
- I've never heard of that
- No, that's not accurate

Ask your witness some questions in a forced-choice format, relevant to your case or not, and give him the opportunity to work on precisely limited affirmative and negative responses. There are countless ways to say these things, so let him find his own language, assuring only that it communicates the limitation clearly. The power of this type of answer lies, of course, in its pinpoint accuracy. It allows a witness to stick tightly to the truth, agreeing or disagreeing with general propositions without giving up the important exceptions.

Do not think that merely explaining this concept will guarantee that your witness remembers how to do it. Most of us are lazy about generalizations in our everyday conversation and have to stretch in order to achieve precision. Give your witness the chance to stretch in this way, to practice this important skill of the disciplined truth-teller.

Now let's look at some examples of the amplified affirmative:

- I agree
- I think that is quite accurate
- That is certainly correct
- I believe you are right on that one
- That is exactly the case
- I absolutely concur with that
- I agree wholeheartedly
- That is absolutely, entirely, completely correct!

In the above series of examples, the tone is one of endorsement, as the witness takes a question like "I want a yes or no answer, Mr. Smith. You weren't prepared at all for that accident, were you?" and turns the reply - from what the questioning lawyer may have been hoping for, a sheepish-sounding admission - into an affirmative statement. The answer flows out powerfully because the witness knows how he feels on the topic and believes the most fully truthful answer to the question isn't merely an affirmative response, it is an affirmative response amplified by his agreement on the matter. It is dimensional, and includes both the fact and the feeling: the whole truth.

Some questions are painted in moral tones, and can have the effect of making a witness sound as though she is being forced to agree that a certain moral value is desirable. Here's our example from earlier: "You believe that people should be honest with each other, don't you?" Many witnesses will recognize intuitively that this question is probably intended to set them up for something. As a consequence, they may become defensive and might even be tempted to somehow evade the question, not because they don't agree with the value of honesty, but because they smell the proverbial rat behind the inquiry.

Speak to what matters most, first. That means encourage your witness to endorse this value, because the truth is that she believes in it, and worry about that later question when and if it actually comes. She can take this moral-value question, answer it in the endorsing style that will feel honest and complete to her, and not feel dirtied by the hint of menace behind it. She should take first things first. How might all that sound?

Q. "You believe that people should be honest with each other, don't you?"

- Yes, Sir, I do
- I certainly do
- Of course I believe in honesty
- You bet, it's very important to be honest
- I think it's the key to success in life!
- I don't just believe in it- I teach it to my employees!

Notice how the endorsement makes the response into a positive statement about her character. Much of the time, you and your witness will know a question like this is coming and she won't be afraid of whatever is to follow. But, whether or not she knows what is being foreshadowed by such a question, she should not let the questioner have moral high ground he doesn't deserve. He's not the only one who believes in honesty, as your witness has just honestly noted.

Let's look at some examples of the amplified negative form of a response.

Q. "You agree, don't you, that a supervisor should always be frank and tell an employee if that supervisor has concerns about the employee's work?"

- I disagree
- I think that is incorrect
- I don't believe it is that way at all
- That is simply not the case
- I absolutely disagree
- That could not be more wrong
- That is entirely and completely wrong

By the use of an answering style designed to transform a rigid yes/no answer into a whole-truth statement, much of the sting is taken from forced choice questions. In many instances, these answers will force a follow-up question that allows the witness to explain.

There are some cautions to keep in mind. The first is that many forced choice questions are mundane, and can and should be briskly answered with short responses of the yes/no, correct/incorrect variety. A dimensional answer is not a gimmick and will fail if used as such. It is actually the natural way to make a truthful response in a loaded-question framework.

Many witnesses simply need to be told that it is "okay" to answer a forced-choice question with something other than a one-word reply, if that is the only way to provide a precisely correct answer. Your witness should have this powerful tool available, but not become over-reliant on its use.

Some questioners will insist that a four-word answer is "non-responsive" since they began by asking for a yes/no only. There are two points for your witness to keep in mind in such an instance. The first is that a question that demands a limited affirmative or negative response can **only** be answered that way. To give an absolute yes or no would not be correct; it would not be true. The question cannot be answered as a simple choice between two poles. Your witness need merely stick to her guns on the point, and she will prevail.

Questions that go to morality or principle frequently need to be answered with an amplified affirmative or negative response because the tone or implication in the question simply demands it. To the witness, a weak response wouldn't feel sufficiently true. Nor is the downside of facing an objection or rebuke a steep one. A lawyer who asks "You believe in honesty, don't you?" and then objects when the witness replies, "You bet I do!" has already lost the point if the witness clearly meant it when she said it. There is little to fear, as long as the answer is genuine and not a manipulation or an act of faux sincerity.

The "I'm Sorry, but I'm Confused" Exercise

Do this exercise with your witness to help him build skills for the management of interference. This exercise should probably be performed with all witnesses who have not had this specific training, as our experience teaches us that even witnesses who have testified a number of times benefit greatly. This is one of the fundamental skills of gatekeeping. A witness who knows how to manage confusing input in questions will have a far better chance of protecting the Truth as he understands it.

Ask him several questions *in adversarial mode* which refer at least in part to facts or circumstances about which he has no knowledge. This can be easy and fun for you, as you can simply invent these "facts" for the purpose of the questions. If there is no testimony of an eyewitness, for example, you might refer in the introduction to your question to the "eyewitness testimony of this event".

As an alternative to inventing facts from whole cloth, you might make up and insert factual material from the actual case that is half-right and half-wrong. For example, if he attended a meeting with Mr. Jones, you might ask, "So, after you and Mr. Johnson (rather than Jones) left that meeting, where did you go?"

The idea is to create a moment of disequilibrium, of uncertainty. You want your witness to learn to recognize those moments and, importantly, NOT feel anxious when they occur. All it is – is confusion. Confusion is not an admission of some sort. Confusion is not refusal to answer. Confusion is not perjury. It is just confusion.

The questions might sound like this:

Question: "So, even with the clear evidence from the Commission investigation, the Safety Board reports (*the witness has never heard this before*), and the opinions of the experts, Acme Corp still isn't going to face the truth, isn't that right?"

Answer: "I'm sorry, I'm confused."

Now, this question has lots of problems, doesn't it? It seems likely that you might object to the question for any number of reasons. However, if you elect not to object, your witness might be able to handle it just fine!

Let's focus on the unfamiliar reference that your witness almost surely noticed, the "Safety Board reports".

Explain to your witness that his first response to a question that creates confusion is to relax and release himself from any sense of obligation to answer it as asked. It is a flawed question and as such is un-answerable. It is the questioning attorney's problem to fix. However, your witness can exert a certain measure of control over the situation.

One way of exerting this control is that which is illustrated above. The witness simply announces what has just happened. He has gotten confused by the question. Now the questioning attorney must decide what to do next. From your perspective this is good, of course, because the attorney has to go "off script" and think on his feet.

In this instance, we are suggesting that the witness recognized what was confusing him. He has never heard of any Safety Board reports. If the attorney asks the witness what has him confused, the witness can explain. Then, if there really are such reports, the questioning attorney has to decide whether to educate him on the issue.

When a witness hears about a "fact" that is new to him, there is a good chance he will begin sub-vocalizing, saying something like, "Safety Board reports? I don't know what he's talking about. I wonder what I should do now?" Hopefully, you will have helped him understand that not knowing what an attorney is talking about is a time to feel *unburdened* rather than the opposite. He can relax. He doesn't have to decide what to do. All he has to do is announce what has just occurred.

Unfortunately, many witnesses become anxious instead and start in with a more problematic sub-vocalization pattern. This type of pattern creates interference. For example, a witness's inner voice can get going like this: "Oh, no! I must have forgotten this! I feel stupid! I don't know what to do! I'm going to look like an idiot!"

This type of inner speech can be very distracting. Were the words said aloud, they might have a very self-recriminating tone. The witness might start feeling anxious or embarrassed. Both the voice and the feeling are interference, of course, and impair clear thinking. Doing this exercise will help to prevent that problem.

The first example above was that of a witness answering with a simple announcement that he was confused by something he heard in the question and which he could identify. Sometimes, though, a witness gets asked a question and feels confused without knowing exactly why he is confused. This can trigger interference, too, in the above-described common forms of troubling inner vocalizations and unpleasant feelings.

In the witness handbook, *Hotseat*, the reader is told about such situations:

"Confusing or awkwardly phrased questions are often easy to misunderstand. The problem isn't yours alone, as listeners will also have difficulty tracking with a poorly worded question. The correct thing for you to do if you find that the question is awkward or that it just sounds "weird" to you is ask to have it reworded. Simply tell the questioner the truth; that the question is hard to follow, or sounds funny to you. Tell him you aren't sure that you understand it, and request that he try again. Both the questioner and your attorney know that you have the right to ask this.

You may be asked to identify the aspect of the question causing you problems. If you can answer that, you should try to do so. However, even if you can't explain exactly why a question doesn't make sense (and you may not be able to—after all, it doesn't make sense to begin with), you shouldn't try to answer until the question is asked in a way that makes sense to you. As noted earlier in this handbook, you should assert the right to be asked an answerable question; that means a question you understand.

Think about this: How can you answer a question with honesty if you honestly don't know what the question really means?"

Help your witness learn to feel okay even when he is confused by a question. Give him the opportunity to recognize such situations and deal with them in a relaxed way. He will be more confident and effective across the board when he can remain untroubled by such moments.

Intervening with Bad Questions

As witnesses begin to get more comfortable in the hotseat, they can learn to exert more control over the form of the questions they are asked. We call this "intervening" with a question.

Successfully intervening with bad questions does not require that a witness learn elaborate communications patterns. Most communications interventions are really everyday conversational devices we all utilize when we want to make absolutely sure we understand one another.

Explain to your witness that we all learn at some time in our lives how to point out inaccurate characterizations and to question the way things are put. We develop at least some ability to ask about new or interesting assumptions when we hear others express them and to challenge assumptions that we think are suspect. We also learn to wonder at least privately over the implications of things said to us, having realized that a strong covert message is occasionally tucked into an innocent-sounding statement.

In short, re-assure your witness that he has probably *already* learned to do or say the right things that make spoken communication clearer. These acts of doing and saying are all interventions. He just needs to learn how to utilize them in this special setting.

The interventions of everyday communication fit readily into the question-and-answer situations in which witnesses find themselves. Applying those interventions is mostly a matter of witnesses learning to do it correctly.

A "correct" intervention by a witness is one that is polite, addresses an actual problem with the question, and either *asks for* or *suggests* a remedy. An intervention with a bad question is not an evasion or a gimmick. It is not arguing with the questioner. It is an attempt to solve a problem.

The goal is to get a clear question, unflawed by confusing word choice or false assumption, that the witness can then answer according to his oath: The Truth. The Whole Truth. Nothing but the Truth.

The "Question the Question" Exercise

Ask your witness some questions in adverse-questioner mode. The questions can be of any style, but you should include within the question one or more of the common problem elements: an inappropriate or inaccurate factual reference, an inaccurate or offensive characterization, an unwarranted conclusion, an unacceptable assumption, etc.

Then, give your witness the chance to practice making a graceful and polite challenge to the question. How? By asking a question about the question. This intervention asks the questioner to provide a solution to the problem.

It should sound something like this:

Q.: "Mr. Jones, when your company decided to rush this machine into the marketplace, you were head of product development, weren't you?"

A. "Excuse me, I'm not sure I understand the question. Can you ask it again?"

The old stand-by: Ask to have the question repeated. Maybe the questioner will take at least part the problem out. But, don't bank on it! This mechanism mostly just tells the questioner that a problem has been noticed by the deponent.

Let's try a variation that exerts more control:

Q.: "Mr. Jones, when your company decided to rush this machine into the marketplace, you were head of product development, weren't you?"

A. "I'm sorry, but I'm not sure what is meant by "rush to the marketplace"?

This mechanism usually forces the questioner to consider defining the selected term in a second and different question. No matter though, the deponent now has a measure of control.

A. "Excuse me, could you tell me what you mean when you say we "rushed a machine into the marketplace"?

This directly requests an *explanation* of the word choice. The questioner has to deliver something on that request, or, as most do, he will move to a different version of the question. In either event, the deponent has affected the moment and, hopefully, will get fairer wording on the next question. If fairer wording isn't forthcoming and the questioner persists with the use of a phrase like "rush to the marketplace", then the witness will have earned the right to "push back" in his answer. He noticed a problem, asked the questioner for a solution, and the questioner refused to give one. The witness is now "one up" in this unfair exchange!

There are a number of ways your witness can "question the question", but make sure you teach him this important rule: Question the question, NOT the questioner. Say, "I don't understand the question." Rather than, "I don't understand you", or "Your question doesn't make sense." These latter personalize the exchange and connect the quality of the question to the quality of the person. This can antagonize some questioners. That is an unnecessary complexity. Next is an intervention that *provides* a solution rather than asking for one.

The "Detect-and-Correct" Exercise

Have a conversation with your witness in which you speak to him only by asking leading questions that contain assumptions. Tell him he should listen for even the smallest inaccuracies in the questions and answer by correcting the inaccuracy. Give him a chance to listen to and respond to them in whatever method comes naturally. The goal is for him to detect erroneous assumptions and insert correct statements in his response.

It should sound something like this (Just pick an ordinary topic, such as his car, and start making guesses which you then embed in a leading question. You will find this easy and fun.):

Q. "Your car is a 2008 Toyota Camry, isn't it?" (A wild guess! You've never seen his car! Press on!)

A.
"No, Sir, it's a Tahoe."

Q. "Your Tahoe is green and has an oil leak, isn't that true?"

A. "No, Sir, it's white and there is nothing wrong with it."

Q. "You are crazy about your car, aren't you?"

A. "Well, Sir, I sure like my Tahoe a lot."

Q. "And you'll never want any other kind of car, will you?"

A. "Not true, Sir. I might get a sports car someday."

In our example, this witness very comfortably pushes back on inaccurate statements offered as facts. He shows pretty refined listening skills, too, as he detects-and-corrects the overstated "…crazy about your car…" to "…I sure like my Tahoe…"

You should stress to him that, when under oath, he should not go along with the use of any terms in a leading question with which he does not 100% agree. He should disagree with those terms and politely submit different language with the same kind of relaxed correcting response that he uses here.

It is in this "pushing-back" component of testimony where politeness on the part of a witness really matters. Notice in the example, that our witness addresses the attorney as "Sir" in every answer. Doing it this way in the exercise helps him train himself to contradict a questioner (if he must) in a courteous manner. It might sound a bit formal, but it is always socially acceptable to be *too* polite to an adversary. Being insufficiently polite, on the other hand, is risky. Encourage all your witnesses to make any social errors, if such errors occur at all, in the direction of excessive attention to courtesy. Too much politeness is always better than too little.

After you have done the Detect-and-Correct exercise with a witness, help him recognize the implications of what he has done. He listened to a question and found that it contained an erroneous assumption. He rejected the question as originally formed and submitted a response that essentially corrected the error. It is by doing just that - auditing the question and then correcting it in the response – that witnesses can take a measure of control and better defend their sense of the truth.

Mischaracterizations in Questions

It is well understood in law that it is often not so much about what the issue is as much as it is about how the issue is framed. For example: Everyone may agree that an accident happened. A car and truck collided. People were hurt. But, what *kind* of accident? A *tragic* accident? An *unnecessary* one? An *unavoidable* one? A witness to an event such as this must decide what descriptive language captures the truth as he sees it.

When questioned, witnesses must have the ability to retrieve the descriptive language they have selected so as to testify to the Whole Truth about an event or situation. But, being able to retrieve the language a witness thinks to be most accurate is only part of it. He usually will have to be able to deal with language proposed by a questioner, too.

The "Detect and Correct" exercise addresses what to do when the witness hears clear error in a question. But, sometime the problem is more subtle. Questioners can create a dilemma for a witness when the underlying fact or facts are not contested at all, but some characterization of the event or one of its components is worded *just a bit* differently from how the witness would have said it. Detecting and responding to these differences is an important skill to help your witness to acquire.

An important truth can be obliterated by a lie, concealed by an omission, or camouflaged in a thicket of lesser truths. These situations are usually easier to recognize and deal with. But, truth can also be gently diminished, re-shaped, lit a little differently, or re-painted in the same color, but with a different hue, until it only vaguely resembles what it once was.

During legal testimony, these transformations can be wrought incrementally, even soothingly, by the use of inoffensive-sounding language embedded in questions. This is language that slowly lures a witness away from what he believed to be the truth when he walked in.

Allowing small shifts in the way a fact is characterized can, after several such shifts, lead a witness to the surprise realization that he is sounding as though he has just reversed his view completely! He will be disoriented and uncomfortable if this happens. He needs to know how to protect himself from being "walked" away from what he holds to be the full and complete truth.

There are generally two situations he should be able to handle. The first is when he recognizes new language wrapped around a familiar fact that, to him, *changes* the fact in some way. He need not be able to explain how the fact is changed, only that it doesn't seem quite right when said the way the questioner has said it. Or, when put the way the questioner puts it, the statement is not as accurate as the way he, the witness, believes he can speak to it.

The other kind of situation is when the questioner is using new descriptive language with regard to a fact and all the witness recognizes is that he hasn't heard it spoken about in that fashion before. We argue – and you probably would, too – that in this situation the witness should always proceed with caution. New ways of framing an idea are hard to evaluate from the hotseat. Some of these formulations may be good – even if advanced by your adversary in the case. Novelty in wording can sometimes create unexpected breakthroughs in thinking that are useful to everyone.

But, new formulations of a fact can also be erroneous or even false! The problem, of course, is that the witness may not see the error or falsehood right away. The words used by the questioner may sound persuasive to the witness; seem inarguable, convincing. He needs to know how to gracefully and sincerely manage this scenario. Generally, we advise that novelty be initially be met with thoughtful skepticism; though not knee-jerk resistance.

Do the following exercises with your witness to help him handle the two above-mentioned scenarios.

The "I Wouldn't Put It That Way" Exercise

After talking about this type of situation with your witness, ask him some questions in adversarial mode that include descriptive langage or characterizations which are a little "off".

Give your witness the opportunity to notice and then respond with a polite and effective intervention built around the phrase, "I wouldn't put it that way."

(Variations on, "I wouldn't put it that way" include: "I wouldn't say it like that.", "I wouldn't use those words.", "I would put it differently.", "I would describe it another way.", etc.)

It should sound something like this:

Q: "Mr. Jones, you will agree, won't you, that you didn't have any particular concerns about the safety procedures for the Acme job?"

A: "I'm sorry. I wouldn't put it that way. I would say that we were comfortable with our safety procedure."

Experienced witnesses might break this response into parts that demand more work from the questioner. Here's how that might go:

Q: "Mr. Jones, you will agree, won't you, that you didn't have any particular concerns about the safety procedures for the Acme job?"

A: I'm sorry. No I don't agree."

Q: "You don't agree with Mr. Smith's testimony that there were no particular concerns?"

A: "No, sir. I just wouldn't put it that way. I think there's a more accurate way to put it."

Q. "And, how DO you want to put it, Mr. Jones?"

A: "I think the accurate way to say it is that we were comfortable with our safety procedures. To me, "no concerns" sounds like we didn't think about it at all – and that's not true."

The protocol utilized here makes for a very powerful intervention. Notice that it has three parts:

1) An apology followed by a disagreement.
2) The statement that there is a better way to "put it".
3) A more accurate statement and an argument for why it is more accurate.

This three step intervention pattern can be applied anytime a witness believes that the attorney's characterizations change the quality of a fact, thus rendering the fact less true.

The witness in this example needed to have the alternate characterization "ready to go". He needed to have thought about the topic during prep and come to understand that an attempt might be made to show that he and his company were "not concerned about safety". Most importantly, he must believe that *it would not be the truth* for him to agree to a statement that hinted of lack of concern.

Sincerity and honesty must always lead. Interventions with problem questions are not games. They are not maneuvers or manipulations. They are tools for protecting the truth as the witness sees it.

Give your witness the opportunity to handle a few questions using the "I wouldn't put it that way" intervention or a variation of his own that accomplishes the same function. He will feel greatly empowered by it.

The "When You Put it That Way" Exercise

Help your witness understand that there are likely to be instances when he is asked to accept or to agree to new propositions he hasn't heard before. They will be propositions that sound completely reasonable at the time they are asked, but which, in fact, may not be reasonable at all. Help him to see that he should be thoughtful and proceed cautiously with new propositions or new (to the witness) evidence.

A common scenario that trips a witness up is when he is told that "Mrs. Smith" will testify to "a new fact" he hasn't heard before – and the witness is then asked to agree that this is (or should be) key testimony and thus important evidence. This new material can sound very persuasive at first blush, and the witness's honest initial reaction is to agree that it could be important. Since his first duty is to be fully truthful, he must acknowledge as much. But, then what?

Your witness will need to know how to recognize the situation and apply the "When you put it that way." intervention. (Variations include, "When you say it like that.", "When you tell me that.", "Looking at it that way." Etc.)

The utility of this intervention is that it allows the witness to *conditionally* agree. His agreement is based in the moment and reliant upon what the lawyer has given him. He is reserving the right to include additional information later, to think about it some more, perhaps even to change his mind. This, we must stress, is not a "maneuver". It is *scrupulous truthfulness* of the first order.

Here's how it might sound:

Q.: "Mr. Jones, the evidence will be that the Railroad Manual didn't come out with this particular safety rule until 2014, one year AFTER the accident. That turned out to be a tragic omission, didn't it."

A.: "When you put it that way, it does sound tragic; but, I wonder if there's more to it."

Q.: "You're not going to disagree that it's tragic, are you?"

A.: "As I said, it sounds like a tragic omission, as you put it, but I wonder if there's more to know about it."

Notice the answer protocol the witness is utilizing so that he can adhere tightly to the truth:

> What you say *sounds* reasonable
> I will agree on that with you
> My agreement, though, is conditional; I want to know more (and/or think about it more)

Helping your witness know how to conditionally agree to reasonable sounding propositions will take a great deal of pressure off of him during his testimony. This is an important and useful communication skill, indeed.

You probably noted how close the above question example came to being a "what if" question (As in, "What if an eye-witness came in to testify about this accident?"), which is essentially an informally worded hypothetical. Hypothetical questions can be anxiety-provoking for witnesses. However, as with many of the other aspects of testifying we've looked at so far, the appropriate skills *can* be learned that will make such questions entirely manageable.

Let's look at hypothetical questions now.

Hypothetical Questions

Hypothetical questions create a great deal of anxiety for witnesses (and, often, their lawyers!) because they can work tricks in the mind of the listener. Let's look at an example:

Q. "Mr. Smith, if you had the chance to do it over again, you would have tied that box more tightly onto that trailer, wouldn't you?"

A. "Yes, I would."

Smith probably feels little choice but to answer this way. It is at least *close* to the truth as he feels it. But, there is a problem. It sounds as though Smith might be second-guessing the quality of his box-tying! Is this an admission of negligence?

What if Smith had answered more accurately, like this:

A. "If I had known what I know now, that the truck would go over an embankment and the box would be torn loose and hurt Mrs. Jones; I would have glued, welded, and nailed that box to the trailer!"

In the above answer, Smith correctly re-frames the hypothetical as being considered in the light of *hindsight*. That would be the truth with almost any hypothetical scenarios your witness will be asked to consider. What-if questions in litigation are almost always being considered in the light of a unique event. They are distorted by the lens of hindsight and often colored with the dark tones of tragedy. The witness should say something about this reality as an accompaniment to any answer he might offer. In other words, he should limit his answer with a reference to the role of hindsight. Any response not conditioned in this manner would simply not be true.

Another important thing to teach your witness is that any hypothetical question is bounded by the assumptions the questioner poses at the time the question is asked. The witness might well have used different assumptions, or additional ones, if he had thought of the question, or when he thinks of it later. The assumptions considered when the questions is asked might not make sense when re-considered later, even though they sounded reasonable when the question is asked. Given these confounding truths, the witness can only *guess* at an answer to such a question. When he does answer a hypothetical, he should attach an appropriate proviso, a "guess tag" (as in, "I'm guessing, here, but…") that sounds something like this:

"As I think about your question right here, right now- my best guess is that the answer is X"

or

"Working only with the assumptions you have just given me, I think perhaps X"

In *Hotseat*, the reader gets this additional tidbit on the subject:

"Some professionals (physicians, scientists, and engineers, for example) testify frequently in cases where their knowledge can be helpful. They are usually called "expert witnesses", and are trained to analyze hypothetical scenarios for the purposes of making legal testimony. They may frequently be obliged to answer this type question. They know how to filter assumptions and how to form and scientifically limit the conclusions that emerge from what-if thinking. They almost always attach appropriate limiting language to their opinions. Proceeding extremely carefully and being tentative in answering hypothetical questions is not some form of evasion or avoidance, it is intellectual honesty."

Ask your witness some what-if questions and request that he couch his responses in appropriate limiting language, using "guess tags". This is a skill easily acquired, and he will be much more comfortable if he knows how to do it. He'll be more relaxed and confident, and will proceed with greater resourcefulness on other substantive issues. Guess tags allow a witness to answer hypotheticals in the scrupulously honest and at-the-same-time entirely tentative fashion fitting to this unique type of question.

The "Guess Tag" Exercise

You need not use the specific issues in your case to give your witness some practice in dealing with hypothetical questions. You can easily use the facts of his life to generate what-if questions. To foster flexibility, invite him to use more than one guess tag to limit his answers. It could sound like this:

Q. "You went to a public high school and then on to the state university, didn't you?"

A. "Yes, sir, I did."

Q. "If you had gone to a private college prep school, you would probably could have gotten yourself a scholarship, right?"

(This is a "probably could have" question. "Woulda, Coulda, Shoulda" questions are just as much hypothetical as any that are more formally proposed! Many witnesses never see them coming…)

A. "I'm sorry. I can't answer that. I would only be guessing." (This is answered with a polite refusal to guess.)

As innocuous as the question above sounds, it should be answered with the same discipline as any other. The point is for the witness to learn to recognize these questions. If he wants to answer in a more relaxed way, while still hewing to the rule of knowledge, he might answer something like this:

Q. "If you had gone to a private prep school, you would probably could have gotten yourself a scholarship, right?"

A. "I can only guess about that, but since I had pretty good grades, having a diploma from a good prep school, too, might have made things even better." (Here the witness starts with a guess tag and then makes an honest guess.)

Notice how the guess, if submitted, should have appropriately tentative language (*"might* have made things even better"). This will send the correct message: The precise truth is that the witness doesn't know what, if anything, would have been different. It's impossible to know such a thing.

Rules-Based Questions

Examining witnesses about "rules" has become a popular practice in recent years. The approach is straightforward. A policy or procedure or standard is posited by the questioner. It is one to which the witness is likely to agree. It is then re-stated by the questioner as a "rule". The witness is pushed to agree that it is indeed a "rule".

The witness is then challenged to agree that violating this "rule", like violating any rule, is bad or careless or negligent or wrong. Finally, the witness is made to admit that he or his colleagues or his company in fact DID violate the "rule" and are thus at fault for whatever injury the violation is alleged to have caused. In personal injury litigation, these rule-based question patterns are used by both sides, though plaintiff lawyers seem to rely upon them more frequently. Defense lawyers, however, may also turn to rule-based patterns to establish contributory fault by a plaintiff or to point to the fault of others.

You should discuss with your witness the concept of "rules" that may come up in your case. It will be very helpful for him if he has given the topic some careful thought and formulated a sense of what is true *for him* with regard to any policies, procedures, or standards that may come up. If he is questioned by an attorney who is inclined to rule-based inquiry, he will be greatly aided by having done this homework.

Partly, your discussion with your witness will be almost a philosophical exploration. You should discuss the complex network of conceptual structures that help to guide and govern our everyday activities. If your witness is a professional, as he works he is guided by a number of types of ideas – all simultaneously influencing him. These include standards, policies, procedures, codes, and protocols. Further, he is also influenced and aided by guidelines, recommended practices and procedures, the typical practices unique to him; his goals, work parameters, and performance targets. Finally, he does all these things within the context of the personal and social covenants and expectations around him; the moral, spiritual, and community standards and principles by which he tries to live.

Nobody. Not in your case. Not anywhere. Nobody has just ONE "rule" to follow.

The overlay to this network of influencing ideas is the concept of *reasonableness*. In most legal scenarios, most of the time, people are expected to make *reasonable* efforts, to do or not do that which a reasonable person in the same circumstances would do or not do. Your witness can measure and defend himself by this standard. Put in the simple way we prefer to say it, it usually isn't an open-and-shut matter of whether or not a rule was followed. It is whether or not reasonable efforts were made to follow that rule along with the other rules also at play.

We do not generally recommend teaching legal concepts to witnesses. That is your domain, not theirs. Reasonableness, however, is an idea that can help a witness navigate his way through difficult waters.

Discuss with your witness the *reasonableness* of whatever conduct is in question. Presumably, he believes his own conduct was reasonable; that he appropriately and reasonably applied whatever guiding principles of action fit his circumstance. Help him think about how to speak to it so that he can stick up for himself. If the fact-finder disagrees with the witness, it shouldn't be because the witness didn't know how to explain the truth as he experiences it.

The "Rules" Exercise

After speaking at length with your witness about this general topic, give him the chance to answer some questions. The goal here is for you to create some exchanges wherein a general rule is posited by you (in the role of an adverse examiner), one to which he *must* agree, and then he is challenged by you (still in role) for having failed to follow that rule.

It might sound something like this:

Q: You would agree with me, wouldn't you, that parents should protect their small children from serious injury?

A: Yes, I think I would agree with that.

Q: That is one of the important rules of parenthood, isn't it, that we should protect our children from being seriously hurt?

A: I am not sure that I would call it a rule. I would call it one of the goals of being a parent.

Q: So, you are saying that its only a "goal", that you don't really have to protect a child from being injured and traumatized?

A: Of course trying to protect children is important, I certainly agree with that point. But, it is only one part of parenting, and I think there is only one actual *rule*: Love them. After that, it is all about goals.

Notice how the witness handles the above question pattern. The response he uses may be recognizable to you as the well-traveled "accept *a*/reject *b*/reframe as *c*" pattern of argument.

The witness comfortable agrees with the general premise but not with casting it as a stand-alone "rule". This is not merely good communications strategy. It is the truth. No rule stands alone, save – perhaps – the one that the witness has chosen to posit.

The witness never disagrees with the important underlying notion, but instead seeks to keep it in real-life context. His management of this exchange comes from having thought about and discussed the topic with his attorney prior to this examination. He has considered the matter and formed a viewpoint about which he can now honestly testify.

This is the general pattern for the initial handling of "rules" questions.

Accept the (usually) reasonable underlying idea
Reject the definition of the idea as a stand-alone "rule"
Re-frame the idea correctly in a more general way as a "goal" (or a "principle" or a "belief" or an "ideal") that is one among many such simultaneously-operating guiding ideas which he, and others, tries to follow.

It is important to keep in mind that the best management of "rules" questions is to refer to the enduring Truth: no single rule governs all actions, all the time.

The day will not be saved merely by reframing an idea so that a stand-alone "rule" is now treated as one "goal" among several. It is true, but it isn't enough. The goal may still stand unmet, and the witness must still speak to it. Examiners can be relentless on this topic.

What if the witness hasn't thought about the topic in advance and is just completely blindsided by a proposition that sounds simple and oh-so-logical? Here's hoping you will have already practiced the "When You Put it That Way" exercise! If you and your witness have done that, you will be well-prepared in the important sense that your witness will not be overly disturbed just because the opposing attorney has come up with something that, upon first look, seems inarguable. He can say truthfully that, right there and right then, the point the attorney is advancing sounds persuasive, but he (the witness) suspects he may think differently after considering it further. If he feels it, he may also want to say that, to him, there is something wrong about the idea, but he can't identify it. It *sounds* logical and inarguable, but something about applying it here nevertheless feels *false*. While that may seem paradoxical, it is also the Truth.

In situations like this, it is remaining un-ruffled by the exchange that is most important for the witness. There are surely more questions to come, and he will need to maintain his confidence and composure.

Repetition Facilitates Retrieval

We are constantly speaking with witnesses and attorneys about "retrieval". Retrieval, as we use it, means remembering what you know. When you need some information, you reach into the storage banks of your brain and "retrieve" it. Repeatedly reaching for information and then speaking about it leads to the establishment of well-grooved retrieval pathways. The knowledge is there, at your fingertips. The secret to fostering ready retrieval is repetition.

A witness who is repeatedly asked to describe an event or process from different angles begins to have the memory (and the words to describe it) stored in a convenient "place". He doesn't have to search for the facts or the language needed to answer a question. Importantly, developing ready retrieval is much different from mere memorizing, which can be an artificial thing that freezes words and ideas into a fixed state. Instead, it is an organizing process that keeps knowledge available and allows for flexible thought.

Memorizing facts isn't in and of itself wrong, assuming that what is memorized is the truth. Recall that many expert witnesses memorize certain charts and tables, useful definitions, etc. They are much aided by having done so, and judge and jury often appreciate the effort. However, the more nuanced material of an expert opinion will rarely have been memorized. It will have been thought about and spoken of a great deal and the witness will have organized his knowledge for ready retrieval.

You can help your witness to be an "expert" on himself and what he knows by having multiple preparation sessions and covering the key topics several times. Each time you visit a topic with your witness, you should take it up a little differently; approach it from a different angle. This will help him to develop the appropriate organization of his knowledge. Further, make sure to ask him adversarial questions, hopefully while doing exercises like the ones in this book. We cannot overstate the importance of doing this. He will be greatly served by having to think about what he knows when he must address his knowledge in light cast by the other side's view of it. Further, he will learn to integrate gatekeeping skills right into his knowledge base. At the conclusion of the process you will have what every trial lawyer wants: a confident witness who really knows what the truth is, how to speak to it, and how to stick up for himself under fire.

Conclusion

We hope that you have found some useful ideas in this short book. No doubt you realize that some witnesses will take much more readily than others to systematic preparation of this type. The more general communications handbook, *Hotseat*, can serve as a companion to your in-person education of your witness. We hope you read it, and consider giving all your witnesses a copy.

One other thing is hoped: That you will learn these skills, have this manual ready at hand, and be able to help your witness during preparation for testimony if he becomes anxious or stuck. Let yourself truly be wise counsel in the sense of being a source of wisdom and support. Let yourself become deeply invested in your witness' success. You will both profit.

www.ingramcontent.com/pod-product-compliance
Lightning Source LLC
Chambersburg PA
CBHW070258190526
45169CB00001B/461